FAITH AND COMPASSION

RAGHU RAI is internationally recognized as one of India's most celebrated photographers. A member of Magnum, his work appears in international magazines including *Time Life*, *National Geographic* and *Paris Match*. He has exhibited widely in Europe, USA and Japan, and has won national and international acclaim. His publications include *India*, *Taj Mahal*, *Calcutta* and *Delhi, A Portrait*.

NAVIN CHAWLA is a senior civil servant who works for the Indian Administrative Service. Educated both in India and at London University and the London School of Economics, he has enjoyed a varied and challenging career. In 1992 he wrote the biography of Mother Teresa with her co-operation. *Mother Teresa* was first published in the United Kingdom, and thereafter in Europe, Japan and India.

FAITH AND COMPASSION

The Life and Work

of Mother Teresa

RAGHU RAI & NAVIN CHAWLA

ELEMENT

Shaftesbury, Dorset • Rockport, Massachusetts • Brisbane, Queensland

First published in Great Britain in 1996 by

ELEMENT BOOKS LIMITED

Shaftesbury, Dorset SP7 8BP

Published in the USA in 1996 by

ELEMENT BOOKS, INC.

PO Box 830, Rockport, MA 01966

Published in Australia in 1996 by

ELEMENT BOOKS LIMITED

for JACARANDA WILEY LIMITED

33 Park Road, Milton, Brisbane 4064

Designed and created for Element Books by

THE BRIDGEWATER BOOK COMPANY

Art Director: Terry Jeavons

Designer: Glyn Bridgewater

Page Makeup: Jane Lanaway

Managing Editor: Anne Townley

Printed in Hong Kong through Worldprint

British Library Cataloguing in Publication data available

Library of Congress Cataloging in Publication data available

ISBN 1–85230–912–1

CONTENTS

ACKNOWLEDGMENTS

THIS BOOK would not have been written without Mother Teresa's consent and the active support of the members of her order. The Sisters and Brothers of the Missionaries of Charity in Calcutta gave me their complete co-operation; they showed me their work and shared their vision. They believe, with humility, that the work they perform is so small that they invariably asked not to be named. I have respected their wishes, except where I have felt their names essential to the narrative. Sister Priscilla particularly helped with factual information that I needed at short notice, for which I am grateful.

Many well-wishers also helped in different ways. My cousin, Meena, and Liaquat Ahamed provided me with a home in London, where I was able to complete my research; Liaquat additionally assisted with ideas on the text. Julian Berry and Susan Dailey were kind and helpful in more ways than one; Godfrey Hodgson, director of the Reuter Foundation Programme at Green College, Oxford, made time to discuss related issues, as did Sir John Burgh, President of Trinity College, Oxford, and Dr Drago Štambuk, Ambassador of Croatia in India; my sister Veena Soota in Delhi and Rinku Chandra at New College, Oxford, helped with editing; the latter also painstakingly transcribed the tapes. Mary Cox, a co-worker of the Missionaries of Charity in Sussex, kindly provided me with copies of the newsletters I have used.

My agent Gillon Aitken's confidence never flagged, while my publisher Michael Mann smilingly accommodated my views. My former secretary in New Delhi, Baljit Bhatia, uncomplainingly responded to all my requests, while Shailesh Gautam generously typed the manuscript in his spare time.

To all of them I am most obliged.

My thanks also for the material quoted from *Mother Teresa* by Navin Chawla, published by Sinclair-Stevenson in hardback and Mandarin in paperback, reproduced by kind permission of the publishers; for extracts from *Something Beautiful for God* by Malcolm Muggeridge, reproduced by kind permission of HarperCollins *Publishers* Ltd; and for an extract from *Gurus, Godmen and Good People* by Khushwant Singh, reproduced by kind permission of Orient Longman Ltd.

Through it all, my wife Rupika and daughters, Rukmini and Mrinalini, gave their unstinting help; I was away from them for a year at Oxford, which alone afforded me the time and freedom from pressures in New Delhi to write, with Raghu Rai, this tribute to Mother Teresa.

NAVIN CHAWLA
Queen Elizabeth House, Oxford

FOREWORD

*'Have you begun to pray yet? You must learn
to pray. Feel often during the day the need for prayer
and take the trouble to pray. Prayer enlarges the
heart until it is capable of containing God's gift of
himself. Ask and seek and your heart will grow big
enough to receive Him and keep Him as your own.
Once you have learned to seek God it will become the
means of great sanctity to you, your family and to
those around you.'*

MOTHER TERESA
in conversation with Navin Chawla, Calcutta, 18 August 1995

LDM   Calcutta, 19/5/94

Dear Navin and Raghu

Let us do something beautiful
for God by giving whole hearted
service for the Glory of God
and the good of our Poor.

God bless you
Mc Teresa mc

INTRODUCTION

In writing the text to accompany Raghu Rai's photographs I have had the good fortune to have been enriched by recalling the long hours spent with Mother Teresa spanning a period of over two decades. From these I have drawn my understanding of her spirit. Letters and notes that I have received from her I have used selectively. I have also sparingly quoted from the only notes that she has been known to make. Kept for a few months in 1948, they describe her first steps outside the cloister, on Calcutta's streets, with no companion, money or even shelter she could call her own. Father van Exem, her spiritual confessor who guided her early development, maintained a steady correspondence with me till he died in 1993. I have drawn on Mother Teresa's private correspondence with Jacqueline de Decker, who started the strand of the Sick and Suffering Co-Workers headquarters in Antwerp. Mother Teresa's letters to co-workers around the world have been used occasionally for an understanding of her message.

There is little in this book for those who completely lack the spiritual instinct. For without an appreciation of her religious beliefs and her inner development, there can be no understanding of this woman, her order and her work. There are hundreds of thousands of recipients of her faith and compassion and one need not travel to Calcutta, as Raghu Rai and I did, to know that loneliness and destitution recognize no boundaries but, like the Missionaries of Charity, belong everywhere.

At the end of September 1995, I was to leave the civil service on a year's sabbatical to Oxford University in England. I had last met Mother Teresa in Calcutta the month before. A few days before my departure, with the intention of saying goodbye, I spoke to a Sister at her Delhi convent to find out where she was; with 559 houses in 115 countries at the time (December 1995) she could have been anywhere. I was

'*I am nothing; I am but an instrument, a tiny pencil in the hands of the Lord with which He writes what he likes. However imperfect we are, He writes beautifully.*'

delighted to learn that she was due in Delhi the very next day. At 9am, she rang. Characteristically, she come straight to the point. 'Can you join me today at Seemapuri, where I would like you to see the new developments? They may need some follow-up.' She was aware of my interest in leprosy. Twenty years ago I had helped to obtain ten acres of Government land for her mission to start a leprosy treatment and rehabilitation centre. Prem Nagar, popularly known as Seemapuri after the name of the locality, had grown from a barren stretch into a cluster of neat brick dormitories, workshops and an operation block for

simple reconstructive surgery. Rice and wheat grew on two sides. Everywhere there were fruit trees. For some of the 200 leprosy patients cured — but deformed — it provided a permanent refuge.

Her visit to Seemapuri over, Mother Teresa pressed on with her engagements. Before I left her, I made an unusual request. Would she be able to visit our home, bless my family and say a prayer? I offered to fetch her from her last appointment. She seemed uncertain and I did not press her.

At about 8pm, when the possibility of her calling had receded, the doorbell rang. It was Mother Teresa, accompanied by two Sisters of her order. She looked frail, her back now bent with age. But for someone who had recently turned 85 and who, this morning, had customarily risen before dawn, taken an early morning two-hour flight from Calcutta, and had since packed in a full day without rest, she seemed remarkably buoyant. 'Accha, I'm here,' she said with a smile, and pressed my wife and daughters onto the sofa with her. As always she gently refused the offer of a cup of tea or even a glass of water. Knowing well that the Missionaries of Charity accept no refreshments outside their convents, I did not insist.

When I had last seen her in Calcutta, in August, I had put to her a few of the stinging accusations that had recently been made about her and her work. She was criticized for being far too closely identified with those on the political right-wing. She was assailed for having accepted money for her work from questionable sources. Her answer was immediate and concise.

'I have never asked anybody for money. I fully depend on divine providence. I have only to pray when we need money for our work. I take no salary, no Government grant, no church assistance, nothing. If people offer me money, I am in conscience bound to take it in charity, so that through this act of charity he [the giver] feels peace of mind and heart. How is this different from thousands of ordinary people who come to feed the poor? Everyone has the right to give. I would never refuse them. My intention is to give peace to people. We have no right to judge anybody. God alone has that right.'

During the half-hour that she sat with us we discussed the other charges that were levelled: that the condition of medical care in her Homes for the Dying was rudimentary, that the dying were administered the last rites according to the Catholic faith, that she provided care in order to convert Hindus and Muslims to Christianity. I knew most of the answers; over a number of years I had seen the work of the Missionaries of Charity in their houses, not only in India but elsewhere. Even in the Vatican, where surely there was no need for conversion, she had persuaded the Pope that destitution and hunger existed. Mother Teresa answered these and other questions stoically, with only a tinge of sadness, saying in the end that she forgave those who had attacked her, her Sisters and their work.

My wife nudged me to let Mother Teresa set off on her long journey to the other side of the city, to her spartan convent, so that she could rest for a few hours before her return flight early the next morning. Before she left, Mother Teresa gathered her companions and my family around her and said a small prayer. Her words, as she clambered into the van of the Missionaries of Charity were, 'All you do, do for the glory of God and the good of people.'

As I waved her goodbye, I reflected that it was 20 years since we had first met. She had invited the lieutenant-governor of Delhi to open a tiny two-roomed rehabilitation centre for a dozen elderly folk, an invitation that he had promptly accepted. I had heard and read about her in a desultory sort of way; in fact I had an impression that her work was confined to Calcutta. Curious to meet her, I accompanied the lieutenant-governor that morning.

Nirmal Hriday means Sacred Heart, though the Missionaries of Charity translate it as the Home of the Immaculate Heart. It lies a mere ten-minute drive from Raj Niwas, the lieutenant-governor's stately official home. It was, however, another world that we entered. I recall clearly my acute embarrassment at arriving in a grand limousine for so simple a function. The first thing that struck me about Mother Teresa was that she was very small — about five feet in height, and slender of build. Her face, even then, was deeply lined and rugged, a testimony to her hard life. Dressed in a white sari with three blue stripes, her head was completely covered. Although I knew she was Albanian in origin, she looked remarkably Indian. I observed that this was in part because she wore her sari with a sense of ease, something not many foreigners manage, and partly, too, because her mannerisms were now those of her adopted country. She first came to India in 1929. She said 'Accha', a North Indian word meaning 'Oh' or 'I see', and 'Thank God' a lot, the latter not in an especially religious sense, but as a kind of punctuation mark. 'It's a hot day, thank God', and 'I'm glad you've come, thank God'.

She first led the lieutenant-governor through the two dormitories of the sick and the aged. This section was the Home for the Dying. Here the elderly poor sat up in their cots to greet us with much warmth and enthusiasm. Behind it lay the rehabilitation centre where those who had recovered but had no place to go

were working on looms, making dusters and bandages. Their output seemed unimportant beside their fulfilment, which looked complete. As she clasped a hand here or stroked a brow there, it was difficult not to notice that her own hands were gnarled and twisted and her feet, in rough, ungainly sandals, were misshapen. Clearly her life had been almost as hard as that of those she tended.

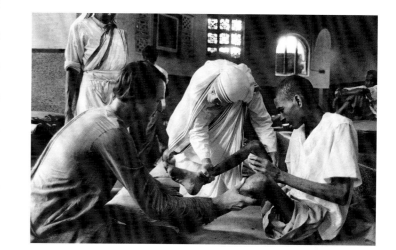

This was not a morning for prepared speeches. Mother Teresa spoke of loving, caring and sharing, of the little centre, and of drops that in the end make the ocean. The lieutenant-governor responded with equal simplicity. He promised to buy every last sheet and bandage, and invited Mother Teresa to visit him, whenever she wished, even without an appointment.

About a fortnight later, when the impact of this visit had all but receded, there was a knock on the door. Mother Teresa stood there, her hands folded in a namaste, *(hands folded in the traditional Indian greeting). I was quite taken aback and it took me a few moments to overcome my surprise and regain my composure. I asked her to sit down for a few minutes until the lieutenant-governor was free.*

She plunged straight into the object of her visit. At many busy intersections of the city cured leprosy patients, who still carried signs of their deformity, begged for alms. Unfortunately, there were not many institutions where they could be housed. If she could be given four or five acres of land somewhere in east Delhi, where most of the affected were living, she would build an institution to house them, treat them and provide skills to those willing and able to learn.

A little while later she repeated this to the lieutenant-governor. She was perceptive enough to see how moved he was. When he asked how much land she needed, she smiled at me and promptly doubled her estimate. The governor instructed me to find her at least ten acres.

That was the beginning of a long association with Mother Teresa. I would try to meet her nearly every time her work brought her to New Delhi and, when I was unable to get to her mission, I would travel to the airport or railway station to see her off. She is particular about arriving early for a departure and this afforded me the opportunity for long conversations with her.

On one such occasion, I asked her about the early days when she first renounced her life at the Loreto Convent for a harder life ministering to the poor on the streets of Calcutta. She replied, 'On one of my first trips along the streets, a priest came up to me. He asked me to give a contribution to a collection for a Catholic press. That morning I had five rupees, but I had given four of them to the poor. I hesitated for a moment, then gave the remaining rupee to the priest. That afternoon the same priest came to see me and brought an envelope. He told me a man who had heard about my work and wished to help me had given him this money. There were fifty rupees in the envelope. At that moment I had the feeling that God had begun to bless the work and would never abandon me.'

Gradually I began to understand how deep and wholehearted is her faith in Christ, whom she sees in every person she ministers to. The first woman she picked up many years ago from a Calcutta drain, her face crawling with maggots, could only be the dying Christ; the infant left in a Caracas dustbin could only be the abandoned Christ; while each emaciated body in the Home for the Dying was the suffering Christ. For

her and her community, it is He whom they tend in every Aids patient they comfort, each child they feed or the urine-soaked body they bathe. As Mother Teresa herself was to explain, 'Otherwise I would be able to look after a few loved ones at the most. People sometimes ask me how I can clean the stinking wound of a leprosy patient. They say to me, "We cannot do it for love of all the money in the world." I tell them, "Nor can we. But we do it for love of Him." '

It was on an evening when my wife and I had gone to New Delhi airport to receive her that a casual remark led to my writing a book about her work. Seeing us as she entered the terminal building, she said, 'Accha, you have come. How are you?' We replied in unison that we were well. With a broad smile she replied that if that were indeed the case she could stop praying for us! We broke into laughter and, delighted, she joined in.

'Mother,' I said, 'none of the books written about you bring out your sense of humour and your joy. I think I should attempt a book.' This was not meant to be taken too seriously. I had never written before — a public report on leprosy that Mother Teresa released in 1987 did not, to my mind, qualify as a proper book, nor did my current job leave me much spare time. Mother Teresa, however, responded quite earnestly. 'There are already far too many books about me. I don't want any more publicity.'

Instead of remaining silent, I replied, 'Isn't a Hindu civil servant qualified to write such a book?' For a while she seemed lost in thought. Then she nodded and said, 'Alright, but write about the work.'

It took almost five years to complete the task, partly because of my work as a civil servant and partly because of the need for extensive research and travel. It became necessary to ask Mother Teresa an ever-increasing number of questions and also to see her go about her daily tasks. I had to track down her associates and persuade them to talk to me about her formative years at the Loreto Convent in Calcutta. I met a number of church leaders, members of other religious denominations, politicians and bureaucrats, journalists and ordinary folk, many of whom were recipients of her ministering. I watched the Sisters and Brothers at work and tried to understand not only what had motivated them to join such a rigorous order, but also their levels of commitment. As an administrator myself, I analyzed at length how a global organization that at many levels appeared to be at least as complex as a multinational conglomerate could be run by Mother Teresa and three Sisters hammering away at rickety typewriters in one small room.

In the early stages Mother Teresa would invariably ask, 'Is the book ready?' Finally, about a year later, I had to admit that I had not written a single word. She probably realized that this was likely to be the venture of a lifetime and never repeated the question. Thereafter, she always welcomed me with a smile and helped with my latest request — a letter of introduction or a few minutes to answer some questions. The only area she was reluctant to discuss was her family and personal life; this she shrugged off as of no consequence. Efforts to draw her out to talk about her mother, her childhood and their home led to desultory remarks and her heart was plainly not in the conversation. She would instead lead me to her current occupations or her immediate plans. On several occasions it would take upwards of an hour to have, in effect, a ten-minute exchange, for there was invariably a long queue of callers. Many came for a blessing — Hindus, Christians, Muslims alike. Others brought their problems. Some wished to make donations. On each occasion she would get up from the bench where we sat to sign a receipt herself or else to hand out her business card, a little yellow slip on which were printed the following lines:

The fruit of Silence is Prayer

The fruit of Prayer is Faith

The fruit of Faith is Love

The fruit of Love is Service

The fruit of Service is Peace.

During one such discussion, when she was interrupted in the midst of almost every sentence, she must have sensed my exasperation, for she put her hand on mine and said gently, 'The doctors don't let me climb down the stairs as often as I would like to. These people have taken the trouble to come. This is my apostolate.'

Having finally completed Mother Teresa in 1992, I had no intention of returning in the foreseeable future to another book on the same subject. But a series of casual meetings with Raghu Rai, generally acclaimed to be among India's best-known photographers, led to his showing me, a year later, his complete portfolio on the Missionaries of Charity. His pictures of the arduous work performed with great love by the Missionaries of Charity against the stark reality of life on the streets of Calcutta are among the most emotive I have seen. He urged me to put a text to his studies. We both felt that it was important to explain the faith of Mother Teresa that lies behind the images in these strong photographs.

NAVIN CHAWLA

PART ONE : THE VISION

' *At eighteen I decided to*
leave home to become a nun.
By then I realized my vocation
was towards the poor. '

THE ENTRANCE TO MOTHERHOUSE, CALCUTTA. THE WOODEN SHUTTER UNDER HER NAME PROCLAIMS HER TO BE 'IN'.

CHAPTER ONE

The Formative Years

AGNES GONXHA BOJAXHIU – later to be known to the world as Mother Teresa – was only 12 years old when she first told her mother she wished to join the Church. Dranafile Bojaxhiu had at that time dissuaded her daughter, for she was far too young. Six years later, Agnes had made up her mind. This meant leaving the security of her home in Skopje, then in Albania, travelling to distant Ireland to join the Loreto Order and finally sailing to the province of Bengal in India, another world away. Her mother knew the time had come. Nor could she have been entirely surprised. Having herself drawn strength from her Catholic faith, she had ensured that her three children were brought up to participate actively in church and parish activities.

Religion formed an important part of their home life. Every evening, Dranafile would gather her family together to recite the rosary. She had consciously brought up her children to be aware of those less fortunate. Regularly, she took food to the poor and was usually accompanied by Agnes. More often than not, the needy were fed at the Bojaxhiu table. When the children were small they often asked who these people were and their mother invariably replied that they were distant kinsmen. Nonetheless, when Agnes told her mother that she had, more than once, received a call that left her feeling deep joy at the prospect of serving God, Dranafile said nothing. Instead she went to her room, where she remained locked up for long hours in prayer and contemplation. Finally, when she emerged, she clasped Agnes' hands and said, 'Put your hands in His hands and walk all the way with Him.' She must have had a heavy heart when she said this for they were a close-knit family; in 1927 India was a very distant part of the globe and it was accepted in those days that missionaries seldom, if ever, returned home.

The influence of her mother and her early life were to shape Agnes' development in great measure, according to Father van Exem. Her deep and abiding faith was, of course, imbibed in those childhood years. Other values that remained with her were to re-emerge in essentially simple acts of charity, particularly to those around her. Her frugality and abhorrence of waste never altered. 'She taught us to love God and to love our neighbour,' Mother Teresa once said to me, a faraway look in her eyes.

Agnes Gonxha Bojaxhiu was born on 26 August 1910 in Skopje. Her date of birth is often given as 27 August, the day she was baptized. In 1910, Skopje was a small town with a population of 25,000, then a part of the kingdom of Albania, itself a part of the Ottoman Empire. Her nationality at birth is often mistaken for Yugoslav, for Skopje, in its chequered political history, later became a part of Yugoslavia. Today it is the capital of Macedonia. Her father, Nicholas Bojaxhiu, was a businessman and building contractor, and a partner in a well-known firm that constructed the first Skopje theatre. He was not of peasant stock as is sometimes claimed. He was an important man in the community and a member of the town council. He spoke several languages, including Serbo-

Croatian and Turkish, as well as his native Albanian. Father van Exem told me that Mother Teresa described her father as a charitable man who never refused the poor. Although he travelled frequently on business, he ensured that his wife had enough money to feed anyone who might knock on their door. A merchant's daughter and an Albanian herself, Dranafile Bernai came from nearby Venice. There were three children: Age, a daughter born in 1904, Lazar, a son born in 1907 and Agnes, the youngest, born in 1910. They grew up in a big house set in a large garden full of fruit trees.

Most of the glimpses of their early life were provided by Lazar when he attended the award ceremony in Oslo in December 1979 to watch his sister receive the Nobel Peace Prize. He described their father as convivial but very serious about Albanian nationalist politics, in which he was deeply involved. The children had their elementary education at the Church of the Sacred Heart. They moved on to non-Catholic state schools and were taught in the compulsory Serbo-Croatian language. Her family called Agnes 'Gonxha', which means rose-bud, for she was pink and plump. She was invariably neatly turned out. She was also the most serious of the three, and although she herself stayed away from whatever mischief her brother was involved in, she never told on him.

Their mother was imbued with a strong sense of values. She spent her time with her children, doing housework or helping others. Her spare moments were devoted to saying the rosary. She disliked waste of any kind. Mother Teresa confirmed an anecdote I had once read about her mother's frugality. On one occasion all three children were sitting around their mother and chattering noisily. As the talk became sillier, their mother, who had been sitting in studied silence, rose and switched off the lights. It was of no use, she said, to waste electricity on idle minds.

Tragedy befell the family when Agnes was seven. Nicholas' political involvement took him one day to Belgrade to attend a dinner engagement. It is suspected that he was poisoned, for on his return he had severe convulsions with bleeding and died suddenly. He was then 48 and in the prime of life. Dranafile Bojaxhiu's world collapsed around her and for several months she lay in a stupor. To compound the tragedy, Nicholas' business partner misappropriated the firm's assets, leaving the widow scarcely more than the roof over their heads. Eventually, however, she recovered. With three small children to rear, she started a little business selling handcrafted cloth and the carpets for which Skopje was then well known. This was particularly enterprising as the Skopje of 1917, after several centuries of Turkish rule, was inevitably a male-dominated society. Her mother's practical sense would be reflected in Agnes in later years.

The Church of the Sacred Heart, more than ever before, became an integral part of the family's life. Mother and daughters also spent many hours reciting the rosary at the feet of the Lady of Letnice, a shrine near Skopje, or late at night in their own home. Agnes and Age joined a number of parish activities and were also enthusiastic members of the church choir. Meanwhile, in 1924, Lazar left home to attend a military school. In 1925 Father Jambrenkovic, a member of the Society of Jesus, became a pastor of the parish; he was to have a major influence on Agnes. He started several activities for young people, including a church library, which Agnes began to frequent. He also set up a branch of an organization called the Sodality of the Blessed Virgin Mary. This was a society for young people that had been founded during the 16th century in Rome and had spread to Catholic communities the world over. It, too, was to have a far-reaching effect on Agnes, for it was a branch of the Sodality that she was to join, years later, in the Entally Convent in Calcutta.

It was from Father Jambrenkovic that Agnes learned about the lives of saints and missionaries and more particularly about the Yugoslav Jesuits who had travelled, the year before, to Bengal in Eastern India. Their zeal to help the abject poor struck an early chord. 'They used to give us the most beautiful descriptions about the experiences they had with the people, and especially the children in India,' she later recalled.

Her deepening interest in the Bengal missionaries led her to join in a small prayer group whose intention was to pray for them and their work. She soon learned that her only route to India lay through an order commonly known as the Loreto nuns, who had worked in the field of education since the mid-19th century. This was an international order and Bengal came under the jurisdiction of the Irish Province.

By the age of 14, Agnes had matured into a young woman. She was always well organized. Unlike her sister, she was not an outstanding student but was confident enough to give a group of children religious instruction; she was to imbibe, early in life, a love of teaching. A cousin recalled that even in those days she refused no one help or assistance and was known to be friendly to all religious persuasions.

When, at 18, Agnes received a call to become a nun, she herself had initial doubts. She prayed at the shrine in Letnice. She also turned to Father Jambrenkovic for counsel. He explained to her that the call of God would invariably be accompanied by deep joy, which should be the compass that afforded the direction to her life's path. She soon became convinced that this was where her vocation lay. Many years later she said to me, 'At eighteen I decided to leave home to become a nun. By then I realized my vocation was

towards the poor. From then on, I have never had the least doubt of my decision.' Pointing a finger heavenwards, she added, 'It was the will of God. He made the choice.'

Agnes applied to the Loreto Order, more properly known as the Sisters of the Institute of the Blessed Virgin Mary. An interview in Loreto House in Paris was followed by her admission to the Loreto Abbey at Rathfarnham, in Dublin. Here she was obliged to spend some weeks learning a little English, the language she would use in India. Her mother, sister, some friends and members of the Sodality travelled together to the railhead at Zagreb to see her off. There she bade a tearful farewell to her mother and her sister. It was the last time she ever saw them.

Agnes did not spend many weeks in Rathfarnham Abbey. In November 1928, she was put on a train to Bari in Italy from where she set sail on a seven-week voyage to Bombay. From there across to Calcutta by the 'Bombay Mail', she travelled the width of India to alight at the bustling Howrah railway station amid strange colours, sounds and smells. After a brief ten days in Calcutta, she was despatched on 16 January 1929 to begin her novitiate at the Loreto Convent in the mountain town of Darjeeling.

Four hundred miles north of Calcutta, in the foothills of the great Himalayan range, Darjeeling served as the summer capital of the government of Bengal. Life in the Loreto Convent, however, was a far cry from the world of the governor and the endless succession of fêtes and garden parties. Sister Marie-Thérèse Breen, a contemporary of Mother Teresa's in the novitiate, described their life there in 1929 as 'an age apart'. The Mistress of Novices was Sister Murphy, an Irish nun who believed that her charges needed a thorough grounding in the habits of prayer and the works of the apostolate. For two

HER DAY BEGINS WITH MASS AT 6AM. SHE HAS OFTEN SAID THAT THIS IS THE SPIRITUAL

FOOD THAT SUSTAINS HER, WITHOUT WHICH SHE COULD NOT GET THROUGH AN HOUR,

OR EVEN A SINGLE MINUTE, OF HER LIFE.

hours each day they taught the children of the poor in a one-room school. They had also to learn an Indian language, so Agnes began to study Bengali in addition to her English lessons.

On 24 March 1931 Sister Agnes took the three lifetime vows of poverty, chastity and obedience. She was now a professed nun. During her novitiate, she had been especially moved by the life of St Thérèse of Lisieux, a young French nun who had prayed with great devotion especially for the missionaries. 'My little way,' she once wrote, 'is the way of spiritual childhood, the way of trust and absolute self-surrender'. Her exceptional goodness in executing the humblest tasks had led the Vatican, in 1927, to canonize her. It was her name that Agnes now felt inspired to adopt. There was, however, a slight impediment. Sister Breen, who had completed her novitiate the year before, had already taken the name of Marie-Thérèse. To avoid confusion, Agnes decided to spell it the Spanish way, 'Teresa', invariably causing people to ask if she had taken the name of the erudite Spanish Carmelite nun. 'Not the big St Teresa of Avila,' she explained to me, 'but the little one'. In the years that followed in the Loreto Convent at Entally, where both Sister Marie-Thérèse and Sister Teresa were sent to teach, the community found an interesting way of distinguishing the two: because of her rapid fluency in the language of the province, Agnes came to be known as the 'Bengali' Teresa.

'I can't say whether I was a good teacher,' said Mother Teresa. 'This my pupils would know better. But I loved teaching. In Loreto, I was the happiest nun in the world.' Since it was important to understand the development of her ideas and beliefs, and the strengthening of her faith during the almost two decades she spent in the cloister, I went to see many of her colleagues from the early days in the Entally Convent. The Entally Convent, located in a somewhat down-at-heel Calcutta neighbourhood, is set in extensive grounds surrounded by a high wall. The main convent and school building is a turn-of-the-century colonial edifice and adjacent to it stands a compact grey classroom block of more recent origin. Sharing the grounds is St Mary's School, a separate institution with distinctive yellow corridors. It was in the parlour of the main building that I met Sister Rozario O'Reilly.

My first impression was of a kindly face, deeply lined and browned by the Calcutta sun. She had not lost her Irish lilt and when I asked her if she was a 'Rathfarnham girl', she laughed delightedly. She began by telling me that she 'came out' in 1938, ten years after Mother Teresa. From 1931 to 1944 Mother Teresa, or Sister Teresa as she was at that time, was a teacher at St Mary's. After Mother du Cenacle (a Mauritian nun who was her Superior at St Mary's) became ill in 1944, Mother Teresa was appointed in her place.

'Our day began at half-past five in the morning,' said Sister Rozario. 'Mother Teresa was always very punctual. We had meditation first, then mass daily at six, after that prayers, then morning duties with the children. She also had her classes, and office work besides. She helped Mother du Cenacle; they worked very well together. Then tea and correction of class work was followed by evening prayers.'

A former pupil at St Mary's who was taught by Sister Teresa was an Indian girl who joined the Loreto Order and became Sister Francesca. She was to become the Secretary of St Mary's. When I met her she was well over 70. As she recalled her childhood, her face lost its severity and her eyes twinkled. 'Sister Teresa organized classes for primary school children. We were all very happy to have an outing. Lots of poor children attended the school. They all used to have a bath after school and, at the end of the year, prizes, usually cakes of soap, were awarded. What a big crowd there used to be!' Sister Gertrude (of the Missionaries of Charity), who was herself a student at St Mary's, was later to say, 'What struck me most in Mother [Teresa] was that she was for everybody. The richest girl in the school wore the same uniform as the poorest. Nobody ever knew who paid the usual fee, and who, being unable to, paid much less!'

From St Mary's my journey took me to the upper-class precincts of the Loreto House in Middleton Row. Here I met Sister Marie-Thérèse Breen. She came out from Rathfarnham in 1928, the year before Mother Teresa. 'We were in the novitiate together in Darjeeling,' she said, 'then I came to Calcutta. When she finished in 1931, we were together again for about fifteen years. But I was not with her all the time…we met at mealtimes, when the community got together, and so on. We did not go out in those days, more cloistered if you like.

'Mother Teresa was very hard working, very. Up to time on this, up to time on that. She never wanted to shirk anything, she was always ready. Always a very pious person, she was just herself. She did not force it on anybody. She just was what she felt she had to be.' After a pause she added, 'She fitted in very well; we were all very happy.'

Other facets revealed themselves. She was a dedicated person who did not spare herself. She was charitable and did not easily tolerate meanness. She could be very firm but showed no vestige of anger. Then, as now, she had a ready sense of humour. When she found something exceedingly amusing, she would hold her waist in both hands and bend double with laughter. Said Sister Breen, 'She was a simple ordinary girl. Very gentle, full of fun. Enjoyed everything that went on. In those early years there was nothing to suggest that she would ever

leave Loreto. We never thought for one single moment that this would be where she would end up.'

While Sister Teresa seldom stepped outside these walls, she was certainly no stranger to the poverty that surrounded her. There were a number of poor children in St Mary's but it was through the Sodality of the Blessed Virgin that was active there that she first had contact, though indirectly, with the dwellers of the adjacent *bustees* (slums). The director of the Sodality was Father Julien Henry, who was Belgian, like his friend Father van Exem, and a member of the Society of Jesus. He was also pastor of the Church of St Teresa and from 1941 to 1946 taught catechism classes in St Mary's. He was, in effect, the school priest and worked closely with Mother Teresa. In addition to the spiritual activities of the Sodality he began a study club, and he encouraged a number of girls to enrol. He believed strongly that prayer without action was not enough, and inspired the group to help the slum dwellers in whatever small ways they could. They made weekly home visits or an excursion on Saturdays to the Campbell Hospital to help with letters for the illiterate and the sick. The activities of Father Henry and his young pupils were Mother Teresa's earliest links with the poorest of the poor.

The tranquillity of convent life was seriously affected by the outbreak of war. Japan's occupation of neighbouring Burma and the threat of invasion made Calcutta the operational centre of the Eastern theatre. There were occasional air raids. Overnight, scores of buildings were requisitioned by the authorities. The Loreto Convent was converted into a hospital and the nuns and students scattered. Some students were taken by their parents to safer places; many nuns were despatched with their boarders and orphans to Darjeeling and other hill stations. St Mary's remained in Calcutta, but was

'Yet not I but Christ liveth in me.'
MOTHER TERESA

shifted a few miles away to a disused factory at 14 Convent Road.

To the desolation caused by war came the tragedy of the Great Famine of 1942–3. The war effort had had the effect of requisitioning every available form of transport; even river-craft, which brought much needed rice from up-country to Calcutta, had been taken over. The supply of Burmese rice, which accounted for 10 per cent of the staple food of Bengal, was cut off because of the Japanese invasion. The Government of India, involved in the war, studiously ignored the early-warning signals and saw the rice shortage as a provincial problem to be solved locally. Prices began to rise. Black marketeers and money-lenders multiplied. In the hinterland, the peasants, already in debt, sold their land and belongings and, in a final bid to avoid starvation, flocked to Calcutta. The Bengal Government proved tragically unequal to the task. Soup kitchens, largely the result of voluntary effort, were woefully inadequate. Millions died. The Government admitted to a figure of two million but many historians believe it was twice that. In any case, so great was the tragedy that its horror has not yet been forgotten in Bengal.

As the war continued, India was preparing for freedom from British rule. Mahatma Gandhi spearheaded the Indian National Congress into a mostly peaceful movement based on his creed of non-violence, using the weapon of *satyagraha* (truth force) that he had wrought to force an end to the British Raj. Alongside the Congress grew the Muslim League under Mohammed Ali Jinnah, also a barrister. The League demanded the partition of India and a separate Muslim homeland, to be called Pakistan. On 16 August 1946 a huge meeting was convened by the Muslim League in Calcutta's great park, the Maidan. The speeches inflamed passions already roused to fever pitch and sparked four days and nights of the bloodiest riots hitherto seen between

Hindus and Muslims. Normal life came to a complete halt as the frenzy of hatred emptied into rivers of blood.

With Independence in 1947 came the partition of India and the creation of two Muslim enclaves that became Pakistan. It meant the division of the provinces of Punjab and Bengal, a thousand miles apart. The largest human migration in history was to follow. Millions moved in both directions, leaving in their wake sadness, bitterness and bloodshed. Refugees poured into Calcutta until it seemed that no pavement was left unoccupied. Municipal services collapsed. The City of Palaces had truly become Kipling's City of Dreadful Night.

It was the rioting of August 1946 that forced Mother Teresa out of St Mary's. She was bound by rules of cloister but, faced with the threat of starvation of 200 children, she stepped out to look for food. She was horrified by what she saw: dead bodies, often mutilated and contorted into weird shapes, littered the streets. Quite by chance she encountered a truckful of soldiers. Appalled to find a nun on the desolate streets, they returned her, together with some food they were carrying, to the safety of the convent.

Three weeks later, on 10 September 1946, Mother Teresa left Calcutta to make her annual retreat to Darjeeling. It was on the small hill-railway train that she heard the call to renounce her life in Loreto and to step out into the streets and slums. 'The message was quite clear,' she explained. 'It was an order. I was to leave the convent. I felt God wanted something more from me. He wanted me to be poor and to love Him in the distressing disguise of the poorest of the poor.'

The call persisted during her entire retreat. In many senses it was a call within a call, a second vocation as it were. She knew her belonging to Christ had not changed, but the prospect of leaving Loreto involved relinquishing a rewarding and congenial life in the convent. It was also bewildering. Although she was the principal of a school, she remained a small functionary in the hierarchy of the Church. Explaining her call and leaving Loreto where she had worked for over 18 years was no easy task. 'I knew where I belonged, but I did not know how to get there,' she said.

Father van Exem, with his prodigious memory, recalled the eventful day in October 1946 when Mother Teresa, just back from completing her retreat in Darjeeling, came to see him. He said, 'She had with her two sheets of ordinary paper on which she had written the inspiration that she had received on the train. I took these with me to the Baithak Khana Church. I was very impressed. From the beginning I had a feeling that it was a real vocation, a real call, and subsequently all that has happened is difficult to explain in a natural way. Mother was not an exceptional person, she was an ordinary Loreto nun, a very ordinary person, but with great love for her Lord... It was not a vision, it was a communication that came as a form of inspiration. She felt distinctly that she had to leave Loreto and start her own work. She has never doubted, not for a moment.'

To my mind, there appeared to be an inevitable progression towards this end. Her family circumstances and early impressions, coupled with her natural inclination, the powerful influence of Fathers Jambrenkovic and Julien Henry and, more latterly, the exposure to unmitigated deprivation, were inexorably leading her in the direction of her chosen vocation. Father van Exem, however, firmly believed that her decision to leave the convent was entirely on account of the call. 'Mother had met poverty well before 1946,' he said. 'This was especially so in 1942 and 1943 during the Great Bengal Famine. The girls in

*The children of Shishu Bhawan, many now happily married
or settled in jobs, constantly visit the sisters. One of the
jokes amongst the Sisters is that a prospective bridegroom
is likely to inherit several mothers-in-law.*

Entally, too, were poor girls. But the call had not come at that time, so Mother never thought of leaving the convent. She knew the poverty of Calcutta and its people and she wanted to work for them, but she thought only of working as a Loreto nun.'

'I had the blessing of obedience,' Mother Teresa has often said. Herein lay an important clue to her development. If the Church had not given her permission, Mother Teresa would never have left the convent to become merely a lay social worker and would, doubtless, be one with her contemporaries in Loreto.

Logically, it was to Father van Exem that she turned for counsel. She had known him since 1944. A member of the Society of Jesus, he had come to Calcutta from his native Belgium. During the disruption caused by the war, when St Mary's School was shifted to its temporary abode on Convent Road, he was asked to offer mass there. Here he met Sister Teresa for the first time and was soon appointed her spiritual director. Father van Exem, well aware that the decision to leave Loreto would finally rest with the Vatican, advised her to apply to the Archbishop of Calcutta, head of the Archdiocese. She would also need permission from the head of her own order, the Mother General at Rathfarnham. She accepted his advice. He promised to raise the matter with Archbishop Perier at the first suitable opportunity. Meanwhile, he advised her to keep her intention secret.

Two months later, when Father van Exem raised the subject, the archbishop was most alarmed. A cautious man, the very thought of a European nun alone on the streets at a time of political and communal tension filled the archbishop with disquiet. I believe it was no coincidence that led to Mother Teresa's transfer shortly thereafter to the city of Asansol,

about 175 miles north-west of Calcutta.

During her absence, Archbishop Perier made several discreet inquiries into whether such a prospect was possible or even desirable. Without revealing Mother Teresa's name, he consulted Father Henry, who although only an assistant vicar was familiar with the slums, on its feasibility. Without realizing they were discussing Mother Teresa, Father Henry was, nevertheless, so excited at the prospect of a nun working in Calcutta's slums that he asked his parishioners to pray for a special intention. Father Sanders, the pastor of St Mary's Church in Kurseong (a hill resort not far from Darjeeling), advised that it was theoretically possible to erect such a congregation. In Europe, the archbishop sought advice from the Father General of the Society of Jesus, who in turn asked the Provincial in India for his views. The archbishop also consulted Father Joseph Creusen, a specialist in canon law.

It took an entire year before the archbishop was satisfied with his inquiries; only then did he permit Mother Teresa to address the Mother General, asking her for permission to be released from the Loreto Order. Mother Teresa wrote in her simple manner, a style that even today remains unaltered. Father van Exem typed it for her. In it she explained her call and sought permission to work outside the convent, by an edict of 'exclaustration', which would permit her vows to remain intact. To her great dismay, the archbishop replaced 'exclaustration' with the word 'secularization', by which, in effect, she would no longer be a vowed nun but a lay woman, a social worker. Father van Exem appealed to the archbishop, but in vain. In obedience, Mother Teresa made the change.

Mother Gertrude's reply from Rathfarnham came as quickly as the postal service then allowed. Father van Exem repeated it verbatim:

31

My dear Mother Teresa,

'Since this is a manifestation of the Will of God, I hereby give you permission to write to Rome. Do not speak to your own Superior, do not speak to your own Provincial. I do not speak to my Counsellors. My consent is sufficient. However, when you write to Rome do not ask for the indent of 'secularization' but 'exclaustration'.

Mother Teresa wrote the application and asked Father van Exem to carry it to the archbishop, who once again insisted on secularization. Dutifully, but with a heavy heart, she again made the change. In February 1948, the archbishop despatched it with his own forwarding letter, to the apostolic nuncio in New Delhi, for transmission to Rome.

Father van Exem recounted that, thereafter, almost every time Mother Teresa saw him she would inquire whether a reply had been received. She prayed fervently. It was four months later, at the end of July 1948, that the archbishop summoned Father van Exem. That afternoon the apostolic nuncio had conveyed the Vatican's permission granting Mother Teresa, not an Indent of Secularization, but the Indent of Exclaustration! In a caveat, however, the archbishop was authorized, after one year, to decide whether her work should continue or she should return to the convent. The Vatican had agreed to allow her to work as a nun in the streets rather than give up her vows.

It was a week later when he was to go to St Mary's to celebrate Sunday mass that Father van Exem was permitted to break the news to Mother Teresa. After mass he asked her to stay behind. Sensing that the answer had come, she froze. Then she asked to be excused for a few minutes to pray. When she heard the news, she knelt down again for a moment of prayer. Her first words were, 'Father, can I go to the slums now?'

The news spread like wildfire in Entally and among the missionaries in Calcutta. Some of her contemporaries were shocked; others, like her friend Sister Rozario, realized the challenge and hoped that her health – always considered a little precarious since she had once had a lung ailment – would withstand the rigorous life she had chosen. Letters went out from Loreto to every one of their institutions asking that their communities neither criticize nor praise, but only pray for her.

Mother Teresa turned to Father van Exem to perform a particularly poignant task. She had written to her mother in Skopje telling her of her decision to leave Loreto, but she believed it would assuage any lingering doubts if her spiritual adviser were himself to explain the call and confirm that her religious vows remained intact.

On 17 August 1948, her last day in the convent, Mother Teresa entered the sacristy of the convent chapel and asked Father van Exem to bless the dress that she would wear from then on. In her hands were three rough white saris, the kind worn by the poorest Bengali women. On these she placed a small cross and a rosary. As Mother du Cenacle wept unrestrainedly, Father van Exem blessed the saris, for henceforth they would be her religious habit. Later that evening, Mother Teresa wore her sari for the first time. It was dusk when she stepped out of Entally. Like her inspiration, the Saint of Lisieux, she, too, had embarked on her 'little way'.

OPPOSITE: MOTHERHOUSE IN CALCUTTA IS HOME TO AS MANY AS 300 NUNS. IT IS PERHAPS NOT UNEXPECTED THAT THEIR DAILY ACTIVITIES, DHOBYING THEIR LINEN OR PRAYING AT THE GROTTO, SPILL OUT INTO THE COURTYARD.

CHAPTER TWO

The Slum Sister

IT WAS FOUR months later that the students at St Mary's heard that Mother Teresa was in the neighbourhood and had started a small school in adjoining Motijhil. A group of excited school-girls rushed to meet her. For children, a principal, no matter how kindly, is a symbol of authority. Instead of the Mother Teresa whom they had always recognized in her nun's habit, they now saw a woman in a coarse sari that covered her head. She no longer wore shoes, for her feet were encased in black leather sandals. And, most horrifying of all, in place of a school as they knew one, they found her conducting a class of half a dozen threadbare children sitting on the ground by a stinking pool, without a vestige of books, pencils and paper, chairs and tables. So pitiable seemed the sight that her visitors burst into tears.

'We began right on the ground,' Mother Teresa was often to say of that period. It was a phrase that would one day go into their constitutions (invariably referred to in the plural) and become a dictum for the Missionaries of Charity. The *bustee* she chose was not an unexpected place to start. Adjoining the convent wall, it was already a familiar sight. The members of the Sodality worked there and Father Henry helped her with the addresses of some families who lived nearby. They welcomed the idea of a school in their midst. She had no money to rent even the cheapest room but not for a moment did this deter her. Finding a little open space near a sump, she gathered a small group of excited children around her. Picking up a rough

stick, she began to draw the letters of the Bengali alphabet on the ground. Her first school had become a reality.

That these early days were hard became abundantly clear from a brief record, in the form of a 'book', that Mother Teresa kept for a few months from 25 December 1948 to 11 June 1949. It is, I believe, the only 'diary' that she has ever maintained. Although a prolific letter-writer, she has seldom been known to keep copies of her correspondence. This account of the genesis of her work and congregation was undertaken at the insistence of Archbishop Perier.

'She was often dead tired and must have fallen asleep many times at her task. I knew she would not have been able to carry on for very long,' Father van Exem said later. The immeasurable value of this book lies in its record of her first halting steps, the unexpected rebuffs, the temptation to return to Loreto and, overwhelmingly, her faith in her call.

Her notes make clear that she had very little money. This was by choice. Had she asked for it, the Loreto Order would have offered her a reasonable sum. When she started her work they certainly helped with furniture, utensils and free education for the early postulants. The first entry in her notebook records that she went to Sealdah (a crowded area with a large railway terminal) to meet the parish priest; he claimed to be 'glad for the work' but offered neither help nor encouragement. There were, not surprisingly, many in the clergy who expressed reservations. The more charitable amongst them felt that the good work that she had done as a teacher was likely to be lost to an uncertain future. A few believed that she had actually taken leave of her senses. Her notes reveal that the parish priest of Park Circus was, however, appreciative of her venture and gave her 100 rupees for the work. Within 24 hours she rented two rooms for a school house right in front of the Motijhil water tank.

While the rooms were being repaired and painted, the school remained out of doors. December to February are comparatively cool months in Calcutta; it is when the monsoon breaks in May that cover becomes vital. Meanwhile the number of children was increasing: by 28 December there were 21. 'The little children were dirty and untidy, but very happy,' she wrote. 'I laughed a good many times, as I had never taught little children before. The *kaw-khaw-gaw* [the ABC of the Bengali alphabet] did not go so well. We used the ground instead of a blackboard – everybody was delighted.' Class was accompanied by lessons in cleanliness. 'Those who were not clean, I gave a good wash at the tank.' On 29 December she noted the children were 'much cleaner'.

The people of Motijhil recognized goodness when they saw it. The chant of the alphabet attracted fresh children almost every day. In a spirit of community service, people came forward with little offerings they could scarcely afford: a chair for Mother Teresa, a table, some slates, even a blackboard. By 4 January three teachers had volunteered part-time services. With their help Mother Teresa began Bengali and arithmetic lessons, and needlework for the girls. By 14 January the schoolrooms were ready, which was just as well because by then attendance had grown to 56.

'There are many joys in the slums,' she wrote one day. 'I had a lovely day with the children – they come, some of them, long before the time and run to meet us.' And, a few days later, 'The children are really improving. They have taken a special virtue not to use bad language.'

On 16 January 1949 she observed that a new family had moved into Motijhil, a Bengali lady with two little children and her sister. They had seen better days but were reduced to abject poverty. In the midst of a class a child said, 'You know, Sister, Zena and her brothers have had nothing to eat since yesterday morning and will have nothing tonight also.' Poor children. They could not say it themselves. 'I had only three *annas*. Well, I can walk from St Teresa's easily. So I bought some *muri* [puffed rice] and the two eggs I had, and made a little meal for the poor children.'

With illness rampant, it was inevitable that she would turn her attention to the sick. Already, on Father van Exem's sound advice, she had undertaken a few months' training in nursing, dispensary and hospital work. Proceeding directly in August to the Medical Mission Sisters in the neighbouring state of Bihar, she threw herself enthusiastically into the hospital regimen. She stood by in midwifery, accident and surgical cases, learned to administer injections and to prescribe basic medicine. The Patna Sisters were to recall that she seemed to be everywhere at once.

The Medical Sisters also acted as her sounding boards and soon dissuaded her from some of her early notions. She told them that she and members who might join her would eat the food of the poorest that they hoped to serve – boiled rice with a sprinkling of salt. The Sisters' practical advice was that if she and her band were not themselves to succumb to the very diseases they hoped to cure, they would need a minimum level of nutrition, however

THE SISTERS SPEND SEVERAL HOURS AT PRAYER EACH DAY.

simple. To rise before 5am and work eight hours, they would need to break the day with adequate rest. A weekly day off was essential and an annual change from the workplace desirable. Personal hygiene was fundamental for everyone who worked in the slums. For this reason, each of them would need at least three saris – one to wear, another to wash and one for emergencies. It would also be practical to keep their heads covered; on an average summer day temperatures could climb to well over 40 degrees Celsius in the shade.

After only a few weeks in Patna, Mother Teresa was raring to return to Calcutta and the 'real' work. 'It was always that she wanted to come back, that she had studied enough, that she had seen all the diseases, that the diseases in Calcutta were different from those in Patna, and that the diseases she would find in the slums she didn't find in the hospital,' said Father van Exem with a laugh. Fearing that if she returned prematurely she might make errors, Father van Exem decided to make inquiries during his retreat in Patna. The Medical Sisters whom he met were surprisingly far-sighted. Sister Stephanie said, 'She is very prudent and will not make a mistake. There will be plenty of people who will come to help and advise her. They will undertake their own responsibilities in the sharing of the work.'

Medical work in Motijhil began, inevitably, with calls on the sick. Tuberculosis and leprosy were rife. 'I met a leper woman,' she wrote on 14 January. 'What a terrible sight. She was thrown [out] by her people on account of her disease.'

An old Muslim lady to whom she gave some medicine said, 'After so many years of suffering, this was the first day [that] I am feeling no pain. Allah sent you to me.' While Campbell Hospital responded promptly to her calls for an ambulance to collect the seriously ill, she began to receive increasing demands for basic medicines. But where were these to come from? In her logical way she started to do the rounds of the pharmacies, urging them to give her what they could spare. Some responded positively, others were less helpful. 'At Tiljala, I got a first-class *gali* [an abuse], but the poor man was so ashamed of his speech… I really did forgive him from the bottom of my heart,' she wrote.

There were many more rebuffs to be endured. Her notes reveal that on 14 January 1949 she got her 'first rude shock'. She had stopped at a church to see if she could get some money for the school. 'What a surprise!' she wrote. 'He [a priest] treated me as if I was doing something very wrong. He advised me to ask the parish priest to finance me. Great was his surprise when I said I shall finance myself by begging. He went off saying he did not understand, and did not say goodbye. It was the first good blow and a hard one. Coming up Camac Street, tears often filled my eyes.' On another occasion, she knocked on the door of a convent for a little quiet shelter where she could eat her afternoon meal and get some water to drink. She was led, not to the refectory, where the nuns ate, but to a space under the rear staircase. Many years later I asked Father van Exem if this were true. He nodded and said that she had seen plenty of humiliation.

By early January Mother Teresa had opened both a dispensary and a second school, providing a glimpse of her administrative acumen. She persuaded the Loreto Convent to allow her the use of a classroom after school hours, which she converted into a makeshift tuberculosis screening centre. The racking coughs of rickshaw pullers and coolies who carried impossibly heavy loads on their heads betrayed their sickness from afar. Somehow she had obtained screening apparatus, and before long lengthy queues began to form. The neighbouring Tiljala slum also needed a school. On 26 January she wrote, 'The children are great. At Tiljala we had only six. At least six little children kept away from idleness and mischief… I got a room for four rupees per month. The people came forward and were very pleased to get a place for their children. This will also do for a dispensary as the children can have their class outside.'

Her notes, though brief, reveal the way in which her ideas were beginning to crystallize. Not for her a preconceived plan on an elaborate drawing board. The usual administrative process of making a survey, gathering resources and training people did not appear essential. She addressed herself to remedying want by the shortest possible route. She could also handle more than one activity at a time. She quickly understood that mendicancy formed an ancient and honourable tradition in India and that there was widespread respect for piety and poverty, hence her 'begging' expeditions and letters. Initially she sought a municipal grant for the Motijhil school, but before it could be given she changed her mind, deciding that 'I wanted to teach the children the things they need the most and I wanted to be free'. Her work started to attract volunteers, but several times there is passing mention of a teacher or doctor who could not attend on a particular day, which would then throw things out of gear. She soon concluded that it was difficult for lay people to devote their undivided attention to work in the slums. On 14 January she noted, 'I went to see the sick but there was too little time and the teacher was anxious to get to her [own] children. It shows how necessary it is that we be religious [used here as a noun] for this work.' On 23 January she observed, 'To persevere doing this work for a long time you need a greater power to push you from behind. Only religious life can give this power.'

After her return from Patna, Father van Exem had found Mother Teresa a room in the Convent of the Little Sisters of the Poor, a considerable distance from her workplace. Sister Rozario recalled those early days. 'Her work day began very early and by 12.30pm she was often still in Motijhil. On her way back she would stop and have her lunch in the school. In the evening she would return to the convent by tram or bus; but there were times when she would offer her tram fare, which was sometimes all the money she possessed, to some needy person. She would then walk the entire distance, which often took her an hour.'

Fearing that she could not impose on the Little Sisters of the Poor for long, she began to look for a room. There were several occasions when she was refused outright or let down at the eleventh hour. A strangely dressed European woman, not attired like a nun and of no fixed abode, was hardly likely to inspire confidence among prospective house owners.

'I went to meet the landlord of 46 Park Circus,' she wrote on 16 February. 'The man never turned up. I am afraid I liked the place too much – and our Lord just wants me to be a "Free Nun", covered with the poverty of the Cross. But today I learned a good lesson – the poverty of the poor must be often too hard for them. When I went around looking for a home, I walked and walked till my legs and arms ached. I thought how they must also ache in body and soul, looking for home, food, help.'

There were several occasions, during these early months, when she was tired and depressed. Sometimes the temptation to return to the regularity and security of Loreto was overwhelming. The work at the convent had, by no means, been easy, but she was devoted to it. In later years she was always to say that it was an even greater sacrifice than leaving home. 'At heart I am

Loreto,' she had repeated. Her notes were candid testimony to her innermost feelings. 'The temptation grew strong. All the beautiful things and comforts – in a word everything. You have only to say a word and all that will be yours again, the tempter kept on saying. Of free choice, My God, and out of love for You, I desire to remain and do whatever be Your Holy Will in my regard. I did not let a single tear come, even if I suffer more than now. I still want to do Your Holy Will. This is the dark night of the birth of the Society. My God give me courage now, this moment, to persevere in fulfilling Your Will.' Convent life was spartan in every sense; 'comforts' must be understood in the context of the hard life of the poor on the streets. Again, on 28 February, she wrote, 'Today my God, what tortures of loneliness. I wonder how long my heart will suffer this. Tears rolled and rolled. Everyone sees my weakness. My God give me courage now to fight self and the tempter. Let me not draw back from the Sacrifice I have made of my free choice and conviction. Immaculate Heart of my Mother, have pity on Thy poor child. For love of Thee I want to live and die a Missionary of Charity.'

It was Father van Exem who remembered that Alfred Gomes, a Bengali Catholic who helped in the Baithak Khana Church, and his brother Michael had a few rooms vacant in their family home at 14 Creek Lane. They were willing to offer Mother Teresa a room on the second floor. Father van Exem felt it would be a suitable place to start. At the end of February Mother Teresa moved in, accompanied by a widow who was a cook at St Mary's. Mother Teresa's worldly possessions fitted into one small box. Michael Gomes offered her some spare furniture, but she accepted only a chair and some packing cases as tables. Father van Exem brought her a print of the Immaculate Heart of Mary – originally her gift to him – which she hung on the wall.

I found Michael Gomes living in the family house in Creek Lane, where he now occupied the floor that Mother Teresa had done almost five decades earlier. Gomes told me of his family's involvement with Mother Teresa's work from the beginning. Michael and his wife often accompanied her to the slums and on her begging expeditions, and a student of Mother Teresa's at St Mary's called Elsie, who had only one arm, also came to help. Meanwhile, Father Henry sent Girirma, a parish worker, so that Mother was never alone in the slums. When there was no one else, the Gomes' eight-year-old daughter Mabel went along with her.

One day, Gomes recounted, Mother Teresa and Mabel had come back late in the afternoon, in the midst of a torrential downpour; they were both soaked to the skin. Mother Teresa apologized profusely that Mabel had got so wet. She then recounted the tragedy they had witnessed. They had found a woman standing in a room without a roof, up to her knees in water. She was trying to protect her child from the rain with a broken enamel basin. The child was burning with fever. The landlord had had the roof broken down because she had been unable to pay the rent for two months, eight rupees in all. Mother Teresa hurried back to help the woman find shelter. Later, someone criticized her, saying that it was not of much use helping one woman when there were hundreds of others in the same plight. She replied that even if what she did represented a drop in the ocean, it was still worth doing, because it would reduce suffering by that one drop.

A few days later, on an equally wet day, she stepped out on one of her begging expeditions. This time she was accompanied by Michael Gomes. The rain was coming down in sheets. Even animals scurried for cover. From the tram window she noticed a man, completely drenched, slumped under a tree. She hurriedly completed her mission – of collecting medicines from a pharmaceutical company – and went back to help the man. She found him, face down in the water, dead. 'Mother was in anguish,' recalled Gomes. ' "Perhaps he had wanted to say something before he died but there was no one there to hear his last words. If only we could find a place where people can die in dignity," she said.' This was the beginning of the search that led to Kalighat, the Home for the Dying.

Often when Michael Gomes reminisced, his eyes half-closed, it seemed as if he had forgotten I was there.

'We would share food with her whenever we could, but I knew there were times when she gave her own morsels away and ate nothing. Sometimes I would get a note from her saying, "Michael, let me have six mugs of rice. I will pay you back." More often than not she would give it to a starving family waiting at the gate. There was an occasion, I remember, when we were in a tram bound for Howrah. Some passengers began to pass remarks to the effect that she was a nun out to convert Hindus to Christianity. For a long while she heard them in silence. Then she turned to them and said gently but firmly, "*Ami Bharater Bharat Amar* [I am Indian and India is mine]." They were startled that she had understood their every word. There was complete silence till they reached their destination.'

On 2 February 1949 Mother Teresa wrote, 'Nirmal Hriday is growing. God be praised for it all. When Our Lady thinks it fit to give me a few children of my own, then only Nirmal Hriday will spread its love everywhere in Calcutta. I keep on telling Her, "I have no children" just as, many years ago, She told Jesus, "They have no vine!" I put all my trust in Her Heart. She is sure to give me in Her own way.'

A few weeks later, on 19 March 1949, St Joseph's Day, a former student at St Mary's, Subhasini Das, knocked on Mother Teresa's door, wishing to join the work. 'It will be a hard life. Are you prepared for it?' Mother Teresa asked. Subhasini, a quiet girl, nodded. She soon changed from her comparatively expensive sari into the humble cotton one. She became the first postulant and took the name Agnes, Mother Teresa's own. A week later another former student, Magdalena Gomes, tall and talkative, joined Mother Teresa. She became Sister Gertrude. Mother Teresa guided her into medicine, leading her to become the Missionaries of Charity's first doctor. In a few months a dozen girls arrived, most of them Mother Teresa's former students. These included the future Sister Dorothy and Sister Margaret Mary. As the girls joined, Mother Teresa began to organize the work systematically. Soon they were regulated by a bell that signalled their times to eat, work, pray or rest. Mother Teresa refused to allow them to give up their studies. In fact she would herself tutor them in the evenings. It was not all work. There was time for recreation, too, during which they played games such as tug-of-war. 'You could hear their laughter down the street,' Michael Gomes said with a smile.

'We lived as nuns,' recalled Sister Agnes, 'but we had not yet been recognized as a separate congregation. The archbishop had yet to approve "our way", and there was no constitution. We did not think of difficulties and always felt God would provide. Mother Teresa was sometimes anxious about food for us. Our tuberculosis patients needed nourishment far more than we did.

BY 8AM THEY FAN OUT IN PAIRS TO THEIR ASSIGNED DUTIES, EACH CARRYING A ROUGH CLOTH BAG OR SOME FOOD FOR THE POOR.

Father van Exem and Father Henry made an announcement at Sunday mass for *mushti bhikkha*, a Bengali custom whereby any family that could afford to put aside a "handful of rice for a beggar". This was the beginning of our feeding programme,' added Sister Agnes. 'Mother was very fond of this custom,' said Sister Gertrude. 'It led us to beg for not only food but old clothes, and even small pieces of soap, so that the poor could keep themselves clean.'

The Sisters ran the schools in the mornings and the dispensary in the afternoons. They tried their best to admit the seriously sick into city hospitals, but often had no choice but to tend them where they found them, in the streets.

The Sisters told me that the Gomes family had helped in innumerable small ways, never charged any rent, and always sent up some food when the Sisters had none. Gomes recalled a scorching summer day when Mother Teresa had gone on one of her 'expeditions'. She had left early that morning and when she returned late that evening, he found her sitting at the back of a truck, atop some bags of flour and rice. She had not eaten all day, nor had she drunk even a drop of water. 'I sometimes hear criticism that Mother Teresa has not organized her work properly, that she does not answer letters, nor immediately acknowledge donations, and that she has little business sense. When they criticize her, I cannot but remember her sitting on those bags to make sure that nothing was stolen and that her girls had something to eat.'

The year of exclaustration ended on 16 August 1949. Archbishop Perier had kept himself abreast of her work and by early 1950 decided it should continue. The only condition he placed on Father van Exem was that the latter should have ready for him by 1 April 1950 a constitution for the new congregation, which he would himself present for final recognition to the Vatican. At last convinced of Mother Teresa's work, he was to give her his unstinted support for the remainder of his life.

Mother Teresa wrote out the initial draft, based on her call. She added to the three vows of chastity, poverty and obedience, common to most Christian orders including Loreto's, a special fourth vow, always referred to by the Missionaries of Charity as 'our way', that of service only to the 'poorest of the poor'. The first signs of this had emerged in her diary, where she had written, 'If the rich people can have the full service and devotion of so many nuns and priests, surely the poorest of the poor and the lowest of the low can have the love and devotion of a few – The Slum Sister they call me, and I am glad to be just that for His love and glory.'

She now gave her outline to Father van Exem, who elaborated on it. 'I took into account the existing canon law, and the constitutions of some other congregations, but most important of all the inspiration that Mother had received on the train journey to Darjeeling and which recurred throughout her retreat…She had to leave her convent and live like the poor, she should not have a big house or big institutions, her work would be in the slums and on the pavements of Calcutta. If they acquired large houses and institutions, it would only be for the helpless, such as abandoned infants and children, or lepers and dying destitutes. Theirs was to be a religious society, not social work. It was charity for Christ in the poor.'

Over the next two years, with 29 young women having joined Mother Teresa, the second floor of the Gomes house resounded with activity. Floors were always being scrubbed, and water for washing, bathing and cooking carried carefully up the wooden staircase in metal buckets. Meals were cooked, lessons taught, and the sound of hymns being sung rang through the

mass for us.' (Quoted by Eileen Egan, *Such a Vision of the Street: Mother Teresa — The Spirit and the Work*, Sidgwick and Jackson, London, 1985.)

On 7 October 1950, the constitutions were approved by the Vatican. No sooner was this done than a room in Creek Lane was arranged as a chapel and a mass celebrated by Archbishop Perier. Father van Exem read out the decree of recognition. The Missionaries of Charity were now accepted as a new congregation limited to the diocese of Calcutta.

house. One day Cardinal Spellman from the United States visited them. Mother Teresa recalled the occasion, 'He asked me where we lived. I told him, "Here in this room, your Eminence. This is our refectory. We move the tables and benches to the side." He wanted to know where the rest of our convent was, where we could study. "We study here, too, your Eminence," I said. Then I added, "And this is also our dormitory." When the Cardinal asked if we had a chapel, I brought him to this end of the room. "It is also our chapel, your Eminence," I told him and I showed him the altar behind the partition. I don't know what he was thinking, but he began to smile. He said

It was soon apparent that the second floor of Creek Lane was beginning to burst at the seams. Father van Exem and Father Henry, ever solicitous, got onto their bicycles and began to search for a bigger place. Suitable premises were suggested at 54A Lower Circular Road, the home of a Muslim magistrate who was migrating to East Pakistan. Archbishop Perier offered to buy it for the Missionaries of Charity, a loan that Mother Teresa was to repay fully over the next ten years. In February 1953, the Missionaries of Charity moved into their new dwelling. Henceforth the Sisters would call it Motherhouse in tribute to their foundress.

CHAPTER THREE

Sisters and Brothers: The Beginning of Their Work

OVER THE 20 years that I have been visiting Motherhouse, very little of its physical aspect has changed. It is true that the wide avenue on which it is located has recently been renamed after Acharya JC Bose, but the clamour of the traffic and frenetic activity at the shops and stalls that surround it remain unaltered. The three-storeyed grey-washed building lends itself to no ostentation, but it is orderly in its aspect. Entry is gained through a narrow lane, wide enough to take a single car.

Most people alight on the main road and walk the few paces to the brown-painted doors. On the wall is a board that reads 'Mother Teresa'. Below it a shutter indicates 'Out' or 'In', but this is often misleading as the street children, playing outside the doors, are wont to move it about at will. In the doorframe hangs a little chain that rings a bell inside, an eminently sensible arrangement during the many years that Calcutta suffered power cuts. On ringing, the door is instantly opened by a Sister or a novice, who leads the visitor to the parlour, a tiny room with a table and a few chairs, none of which ever matches. From the parlour one becomes aware of being in a moderately large building, or a cluster of buildings to be more accurate, enclosing an open space where, in a grotto, stands a statue of the Virgin. Being home to as many as 300 nuns, it is perhaps not unexpected that their daily activities – *dhobying* their linen or praying at the grotto – spill out into the courtyard.

On my first visit to Motherhouse I remember having the impression that I had entered an oasis of cleanliness and calm in the midst of noise and dust. Upon my request to see the chapel I was led upstairs to a long rectangular room whose windows opened onto Lower Circular Road, the name that the people of Calcutta still seem to prefer. There were neither pews nor seats, everyone knelt or sat on the coarse jute matting that softened the impact of a cold January floor. The altar was an unpretentious table. On the walls hung a few framed prints of biblical scenes. On one side of the altar stood the Virgin; at her feet lay a bunch of red gladioli, the only splash of colour in the room. Not only was this the most spartan place of worship that I could recall, it was also the noisiest. Calcutta, like most Indian cities, has a high decibel range, and Lower Circular Road can be awarded high marks on that score. I found it strange that the Sisters in prayer seemed unaffected by the noise of the buses and trams, which when they thundered past seemed to shake the building to its very foundations.

Then, as now, the Sisters rose before dawn, usually by 4.30am. Mass at 6am is preceded by half an hour of meditation, followed by an hour for housework, then a breakfast of tea and chapattis. By 8am they fan out to their assigned duties. Some Sisters head for Shishu Bhawan down the road, others to Kalighat or Prem Dan, the home for elderly inmates, many of whom are those who have recovered in Kalighat but have nowhere to go. Others attend their teaching posts in their many little schools that dot the city. Some ride in the mobile dispensaries as they head for their scheduled stations. Most of them proceed to their allocated streets and slums looking for those in distress. They invariably head out in pairs. Father van Exem was to explain that the reason for the Rule of Two lay as much in personal safety as utility. Mother Teresa put it another way when she said, 'The Lord in the Gospel sent his apostles two by two.' They each carry a rough grey cloth bag, which usually contains a recycled plastic bottle full of water. More often than not, there is a rosary in their hands; for they pray as they go along. On one occasion in Rome, when I accompanied two young Sisters on their way to see an Aids patient, I inquired how far we had to walk. They answered in unison that it was five rosaries away. On seeing my bewilderment they explained, laughing, that praying by rosary as they walked helped to cover the distance more rapidly.

The Sisters return at about 12.30 for lunch, usually a lentil soup, sometimes some meat, and at least four chapattis. The advice offered by the Patna Medical Sisters regarding their diet has been faithfully followed by Mother Teresa. They rest for half an hour before beginning another round of work. Some afternoons they are assigned different tasks in order to vary the routine. Novices remain behind for classes on theology, scriptures and the constitutions. By 6.30 they must all assemble for adoration for a full hour, then recreation, supper and another half hour of prayer. Thursday is the day for rest, for catching up with their religious studies, for washing and household chores. Earlier their three saris were assigned for wearing, washing and special occasions. It is a testimony to their arduous work that the third is now used for darning. I have never yet seen Mother Teresa's own without several patches, neatly darned.

In an age when vast amounts of money are spent on advertising products, which we are repeatedly told we cannot live without, the Sisters choose to receive not much more than a cheap metal-rimmed plate for food, a mug for water, a bucket for washing their clothes, a thin mattress and a pair of sturdy sandals. The only ceiling fan in Motherhouse is for visitors in the parlour; there is neither an oven nor a washing machine, no television, not even a radio. These and many other gadgets have been offered scores of times but

RICKSHAW PULLERS AT
REST ON A CALCUTTA STREET.

always to be refused. When I asked Mother Teresa why she would not at least accept a radio, for the Sisters to know better what was going on in the world, she replied carefully that they 'had the reality'. I was thankful that she had (after much reflection and prayer) agreed to one telephone being installed in each of her principal missions. In spite of Calcutta's archaic phone system (much improved in recent years), it has often surprised me that the phone in Motherhouse has almost never been out of order, a small miracle in itself!

It was as much Mother Teresa's faith as the special appeal she had for her students that attracted the earliest postulants. Sister Agnes, the former Subhasini Das, was the only one of Mother Teresa's students in St Mary's who had some inkling that her principal would one day leave the convent. 'You have often spoken about the need to start this kind of work,' Subhasini Das had once said to Mother Teresa. 'We are ready to help, but we need a leader. Why can't you be our leader?' Mother Teresa had hushed her into silence with a smile. Years later, I asked Sister Agnes whether her family had objected to such an uncertain future. 'My mother was very upset,' she confessed. 'Although she lived in Calcutta, she did not come to see me [for four years]. It took a long time before she could accept.' Were they eventually reconciled? She nodded, somewhat absentmindedly, her thoughts on that fateful morning of March 1949 when she had knocked at Mother Teresa's door in Creek Lane. 'On that day, I entered into my new life, which has brought me only happiness in serving God.'

Mother Teresa devoted as much time as she could spare from her work in the streets to the religious formation of her flock, a practice she has always maintained. Initially, Father van Exem and Father Henry gave the first set of young women the preparation that they felt was needed before they could take their vows. In due course, Mother Teresa and the senior Sisters took on the task. Ever since, new entrants have always been given a thorough grounding in spiritual studies, without the understanding of which, Mother Teresa has often said, their work would be no different from that of social workers. In so saying, she has not deprecated social work, but has emphasized that theirs is a religious path: 'to find Jesus in the distressing disguise of the poorest of the poor as we find Him in the appearance of bread in the eucharist'.

The women who apply to join the society must satisfy four unusual pre-conditions. The aspirants must be healthy of mind and body. They should have the ability to learn. They need to have plenty of common sense and, just as importantly, a cheerful disposition. They enter as 'come-and-sees' for a few weeks or months, to see if the vocation is right for them. Some find the life difficult, others return to their homes, and some wish to get married. The women who choose to remain are aware that they must sever their ties with their families. They are rarely allowed to return home: once every ten years, or if a parent is seriously ill, or before they are sent on a mission abroad.

Upon joining, a girl spends her first six months as an aspirant, and the following half year as a postulant. Some leave at this stage. Others begin a novitiate for two years during, or after, which they are free to leave without special permission. Those who remain take their first vows. What follows is a five-year period the Sisters call the juniorate. Each year they renew their vows to strengthen their spiritual commitment. Once they begin to take their vows they need the permission of the head of the order before they can leave. The sixth year is called the tertianship. Before they take their final vows, they are sent home to their families to reflect on whether they are ready to undertake a life of such tremendous dedication.

Some Missionaries of Charity have left after taking final vows, but the numbers are not large; in fact many more queue up to join. It is this that has permitted Mother Teresa to open an increasing number of homes, as they call their convents and institutions, as well as to expand into new areas of work such as care for patients suffering from Aids. At a time when religious orders of all denominations are easing their rules in order to attract entrants to a life of the spirit, Mother Teresa has made practically no concessions over the almost 50 years that her order has flourished in a spirit of such vigorous self-abnegation. I once asked her what she expected of her Sisters. She replied, 'Let God radiate and live His life in her and through her in the slums. Let the sick and suffering find in her a real angel of comfort and consolation. Let her be the friend of the little children in the street.' Then, with a smile she added, 'I would much rather they make mistakes in kindness than work miracles in unkindness.'

In the parlour at Motherhouse a hand-drawn chart lists the range of their activities, which include child welfare and educational schemes, feeding programmes, day crèches, natural family planning centres, dispensaries, leprosy clinics, rehabilitation centres, homes for abandoned, crippled and mentally retarded children, for unwed mothers and for sick and dying destitutes. A separate column indicates the total number of institutions and those benefited. The figures are frequently out of date because the work has expanded more rapidly than the means of communication available to update the chart! In Western Europe and the United States the emphasis lies mainly on family visiting and prison visiting; institutions here include homes for alcoholics, night shelters, soup kitchens and hospices for Aids patients.

Although the Missionaries of Charity are at work in many countries, there persists the impression that Mother Teresa's activities are confined to Calcutta. Many people are astonished to learn that she has a presence in the West. One reason for this is that neither the Missionaries of Charity nor co-workers are permitted to raise funds. Fundraising makes a charity known; but as this activity is specifically forbidden by Mother Teresa, the usual route of advertising their presence through the press, radio and television is not available. Co-workers and volunteers are instead encouraged to spend their time helping the Sisters or providing succour in their neighbourhoods. Mother Teresa has invariably depended on providence for the needs of her mission. There were scores of occasions, particularly in the early years, when the Sisters would have no money to buy even a little *dal* (lentils) for the children at Shishu Bhawan. On such days they would all eat a handful of rice sprinkled with a little salt. After she became better known, the problem of money for basic needs receded. With the influx of charity came a substantial expansion of her activities, at first in India and, a few years later, overseas.

For the first ten years, however, the work was confined to Calcutta. This was in accordance with canon law, which forbade the opening of new houses outside the diocese by an institute less than ten years old. Well before the decade was out, Mother Teresa was already anxious to open a convent in Ranchi, where a number of her early Sisters had come from, who had convinced her of the need for a home in that largely tribal area. Archbishop Perier, however, gave permission only after the stipulated period was over. A house in Ranchi was followed in quick succession by a Shishu Bhawan in Delhi. This was formally opened by no less than India's then prime minister, Jawaharlal Nehru. 'When I asked him whether I could tell him about our work,' she recounted, 'he replied, "No, Mother, you need not tell me. I know about it. That is why I have come." ' In 1960 Mother Teresa's work began in half a dozen cities and towns. By the end of the 1960s this had grown to 25 houses in India. Two decades later there were 86. By the end of 1995 there were as many as 189 houses in India.

In February 1965 the society became a congregation by pontifical right. Having thus been placed directly under the Vatican, it became possible to open convents and institutions overseas. The idea of going abroad had sprung from the papal nuncio in New Delhi, Archbishop Knox, who persuaded Mother Teresa that the plight of landless people of African descent in Venezuela needed her particular attention. Then she received an invitation from the local bishop and, following this, she went to assess the situation for herself. (This procedure henceforth became her invariable practice for opening a house overseas.) The fact that she now had 300 Sisters also enabled her to respond with more flexibility to the great need she saw in Cocorote in Venezuela. The first four Sisters she sent overseas were all Indian girls. Her next overseas house, in 1968, was not in a Third World country. She saw hunger and destitution in Rome and opened a house in the suburbs of San

Stefano. The following year the special problems of alcoholics and drug addicts in Melbourne, and the poverty of the aborigines in Bourke, led her to open two houses in Australia. In Melbourne she heard of the plight of an elderly man living all alone in a big house. When she visited him, she saw that his room had not been cleaned for a long time. Characteristically, she took duster and brush and began to clean and scrub. Although there was a fine lamp in the room, the light was switched off. To her question, he replied that he had no one to light it for. 'Will you light it if the Sisters visit you?' she asked. 'Yes,' he replied, 'I will light it if I hear the sound of a human voice.'

Houses overseas followed in rapid succession: London, Jordan, New York, Bangladesh, Northern Ireland, the Gaza strip, Yemen, Ethiopia, Sicily, Papua New Guinea, Mexico, the Philippines, Panama, Japan, Portugal, Brazil, Burundi and many others. She found the need for more stations in the USA, which she set up in St Louis, Detroit, Miami, Washington DC, Newark, Appalachia, Chicago and San Francisco. She found great deprivation in some areas of New York and opened homes in Harlem and the Bronx. Additional houses were added in London. In Rome she persuaded Pope John Paul II to give her some rooms to start a soup kitchen in the shadows of St Peter's itself.

In some cases sheer persistence paid off. For years, anxious to open a house in the then USSR, she had petitioned officials at the Soviet embassy in New Delhi. Not one to give up easily, she wrote letters to President Mikhail Gorbachev, but received no reply. She even sent him a congratulatory

MOTHER TERESA ON A VISIT TO A LEPROSY
CENTRE IN THE NORTH-EAST OF INDIA.

telegram on St Michael's Day, which she hoped might serve as a gentle reminder! Permission came unexpectedly in the wake of tragedy. After the devastating earthquake on 7 December 1988 in Armenia, Mother Teresa immediately offered to fly in her Sisters in a relief mission with medicines, clothes and equipment. This was gratefully accepted. The rest followed easily enough and soon there were a number of houses in the former Soviet Union, Eastern Europe and, finally, the country of her birth, Albania.

I have heard from fellow administrators in India, who have been stationed in areas where calamity has struck, that Mother Teresa and her Sisters are able to organize their relief operations efficiently and without fuss. On one occasion I asked Mother Teresa how she went about this. She seemed amused by my question and replied, 'We have plenty of practice, no? For the last thirty-six years that's what we have been doing.' We both laughed. She continued, 'Any time something happens, we are there. We know what people need, and we start doing it. During floods, the Sisters collect food, while the Government provides helicopters to deliver it. Many organizations come forward to help. People give. They help. If everybody does something then the work is done.'

Many of her Sisters are now fully trained doctors or nurses. From the beginning, when she encouraged Sister Gertrude to complete her medical training, she had understood the need for having as many trained doctors and nurses as possible. She herself always felt indebted to the Medical Mission Sisters for the training they had given her. Once, while discussing her Patna days, I remembered a story I had read about her very first surgical case on a Calcutta street. According to this account, she had found a man with a gangrenous thumb that needed immediate amputation. Thereupon she said a prayer, took out a pair of scissors and cut it off. The patient promptly fainted,

falling in one direction while Mother Teresa fainted in the other! When I delivered the punchline, Mother Teresa bent double with laughter. 'A made-up story,' she said, but thoroughly enjoyed the joke!

Mother Teresa's daily routine has not varied as much over the years as one might expect. Like her Sisters she, too, wakes at 4.30am. Her day begins with mass at 6am. She has often said that this is the spiritual food that sustains her, without which she could not get through even an hour of her life.

'In the mass we have Jesus in the appearance of bread, while in the slums I see Christ in the distressing disguise of the poor. The eucharist and the poor are but one love for me,' she has explained. On an average day in Calcutta, Mother Teresa might visit one of her existing institutions or inspect a building, or a site for a new one. She might go to Writers' Building, the state government secretariat, to extract some concession from her friend Jyoti Basu, the communist chief minister of West Bengal, or she might be persuaded by someone in distress to visit a family and say a prayer. She is a great favourite with local schools and colleges. Although she invariably makes much the same speech, her presence ensures a full hall and tickets are usually sold out well in advance. At Motherhouse there is a steady stream of visitors throughout the day, to most of whom she listens patiently. After the day is done, at 9pm or a little later, Mother Teresa retreats into her small office to attend to urgent papers, administration and correspondence. Until her illness in December 1989, when she developed a cardiac ailment, she worked at her desk till the early hours of the morning. She still puts in a couple of hours. It is simply not possible for her to see the hundreds of letters that pour in each day, but her small secretariat under the charge of Sister Priscilla, one of the four councillors general, places on her desk all the letters that they feel need her attention. She answers as many as she can, more often than not in her own hand. (After Mother Teresa herself, the present office bearers are Sister Frederick, a Maltese nun, who is the first councillor and assistant general, followed by Sister Joseph Michael, Sister Priscilla and Sister Monica as the second, third and fourth councillors general. Sister Margaret Mary is the secretary general and Sister Joelle is the treasurer. They are nearly all Indian nuns. While they are office bearers, they are not necessarily the oldest or earliest nuns to join the Missionaries of Charity.)

Anyone who has visited Motherhouse will testify to its air of frugality. Mother Teresa has been careful to maintain her avowed poverty without concession. There is no vestige of comfort. The furniture is spartan but clean. Wherever possible small benches substitute for chairs. During mass, one early January morning, when it is usually quite dark, I noticed that only half the number of lights were switched on. During the next hour light gradually began to filter in through the windows. Although deep in prayer, Mother Teresa would rise every 15 minutes to switch off two lights at a time, until nearer 7am she had instinctively switched them all off. A few days later, while sitting with her on one of the benches in the passage leading to her office, I asked why there was such a weak light, a bulb so feeble I could scarcely make my notes. There was utter seriousness in her reply. 'The money I get is sacrifice money, not money for business. The people who give it sacrifice a lot. They buy cheaper clothes, go without meals.'

She told me about a young Hindu couple who loved each other so much that they wanted to share their love with her and the poor she served. So they went against tradition by doing without a bridal sari and even a wedding feast. Instead they gave her the money that they had saved. She continued, 'Did I tell you about a little boy of three in Calcutta? Where he had heard about Mother Teresa, I don't know, but one day he said to his father that he wanted to give his money to me for the poor. So he asked his father that if he didn't eat sugar, which he loved, for a few days, how much money would be saved? The little boy did not eat sugar for three days. Then he came to me with his father and gave me one rupee. That little child gave until it hurt.'

It is these stories that are etched in Mother Teresa's memory. The large behests and awards that her work attracts are undeniably useful but not ones that touch her. Her essential attitude to money has never changed. If God intends her to do some work, He must provide. The converse holds equally true. There is criticism in some quarters that she could stretch her funds further or use them more purposefully. She could make wise investments and double and triple them. She has rejected these suggestions before and will doubtless reject them again. She is clear that such an approach would convert charity into business. 'I do not need money in a bank,' she said, when she once told me about an Indian millionaire who had offered her a large amount but permitted her to touch only the interest. She had declined this, saying that the collection of money was not the purpose of her work. She then turned to me meaningfully and said, 'The meaning of my life is my love for God. It is Christ I serve in His distressing disguise of the poor. Jesus said, "I was hungry and you gave me food. I was sick and you visited me. Whatsoever you do to the least of my brethren, you do it to me."' Then taking my hand, as she had done so many times before, she slowly repeated with emphasis, 'You – did – it – to – me'. And with each word she pressed my fingers, one by one, into the palm of my hand. Then with a joyful smile, her head on one side, her manner so endearingly childlike, she added: 'Beautiful, no?'

MOTHER TERESA AND HER SISTERS TRAVELLING TO
A MEDICAL CAMP. NOVICES WEAR WHITE SARIS
WITHOUT THE FAMILIAR BLUE STRIPES.

While it is commonplace in Calcutta and other large cities to see the Missionaries of Charity Sisters walking down a street or riding an ambulance, their shining white saris with their three blue bands across their heads recognizable from afar, the Missionaries of Charity Brothers are harder to spot. They are fewer in number, but the main reason is that they wear no distinctive uniform. Although some of them are priests, they dress in ordinary shorts and trousers. It is only when one is face-to-face with them that one notices a small crucifix pinned to their shirts. In Calcutta, more often than not, they can be spotted at the two main railway terminals, Howrah and Sealdah. Here, under the station's cavernous roofs, live scores of young men and boys, eking out their living by running small errands for passengers, or as shoe-shine boys; some even pick the occasional pocket, a rather more profitable but dangerous occupation as it often lands them in jail. For many of these boys – orphaned, abandoned or runaways – the Brothers are their only life-line to a daily hot meal, an occasional game of football or more stable employment.

The fact that the boys in Shishu Bhawan were growing up and the Sisters would soon have difficulty looking after them, coupled with the realization that men were better suited to certain kinds of work, led Mother Teresa to set up a Brothers branch in 1963. They would devote themselves largely to the concerns of older boys and men, as well as perform tasks that needed longer and more flexible hours. Mother Teresa had once again sought Father van Exem's advice, who in turn took her plan for a Brothers congregation to Archbishop Albert Vincent. His response was immediate and positive: 'I want Brothers. Tell Mother Teresa to begin,' he said. Father van Exem was told to send Mother Teresa suitable volunteers to start the work. There were several amusing moments as the Sisters tried to channel the energies of these exuberant young men and Sister Gertrude, who strangely enough knew some carpentry, tried to teach them to make tables and chairs. Mother Teresa, meanwhile, realized that these strapping fellows needed exercise and so she occasionally took them to play volleyball! There were, however, more serious problems. Men were reluctant to join until the Brothers became a regular institute. In turn, recognition from Rome depended on the achievement of sufficient numbers and proper organization. Unexpectedly, Mother Teresa chanced upon a young Australian Jesuit, Ian Travers-Ball. He had been working in Bihar since 1954 and had got permission from his order to spend a month observing the work of the fledgling Missionaries of Charity Brothers at Shishu Bhawan. Ian Travers-Ball was moved by their simplicity and realized the need for a priest to help them with their spiritual growth. At the end of the month, when Mother Teresa asked him to stay and head the congregation, he accepted. Ian Travers-Ball realized that this would mean a clean break from the Jesuit Order. He took the name of Brother Andrew and the title of General Servant.

When I went to visit Brother Andrew one evening, the main meal at 7 Mansatala Row had just ended. I could hear a great deal of shouting and clapping as I climbed the stairs to the top of the small building in a rundown Calcutta street. It was the start of recreation hour, explained Brother Andrew, and this was the way the young men let off steam.

Brother Andrew spoke to me about how their order began and why they had needed to leave Shishu Bhawan. 'I felt the Brothers needed to develop their own leadership and in their own style. We could draw inspiration and support from Mother Teresa, but we needed to function autonomously. Mother entirely agreed.'

He continued, 'Mother bought [this house] for us. There were fifteen of us when we moved in. The lifestyle of a group of men would necessarily be different from that of women. We could not, for instance, live on top of each other the way women have managed to do. Men need to go out for a walk, or have a game of football on a Sunday afternoon. The Sisters don't go out for anything except their work. Household arrangements, too, could not be the same for us.' Although they pursued the same goals, the two branches were clearly to develop separate identities. Mother was to say of him, 'We are so different, but both of us have the same mind.'

The constitutions of this order spelled out their chosen tasks. 'The special aim of the society is to live this life of love by dedicating oneself to the service of the poorest of the poor in the slums, in the streets, and wherever they are to be found. Leprosy patients, destitute beggars, the abandoned, homeless boys, young men in the slums, the unemployed and those uprooted by way and disaster will always be the special object of the Brothers' concern.'

The Brothers began their work at Howrah Railway Station. Hundreds of young boys, including orphans and those who had jumped probation, had made this their home. Disease was commonplace. The Brothers began in small ways. They encouraged the boys to keep clean and presented them with cakes of soap. When they themselves became better organized, they started preparing a hot evening meal for them at Mansatala Row. Gradually they established a special home for homeless and handicapped boys, appropriately naming it *Nabo Jeevan* (New Life). The need to equip these boys with some kind of vocational training led to the start of a workshop in Dum Dum, where basic radio repairs were taught. Many of the boys and young men were tubercular and some were mentally disabled. Brother Andrew set about

acquiring a farm some 20 miles from Calcutta, and here he engaged these young men in agricultural work or simple tasks like making candles and envelopes.

Brother Andrew told me that Mother Teresa had favoured a uniform and many Brothers wanted it too, but he was not convinced. 'I believe that without a uniform we are one with the poor and underprivileged,' he said. However, he accepted the need for women to wear a special dress, for it afforded them a form of identification.

Although the Brothers began to work in spheres where the Sisters were largely absent, there were some areas where they shared the work. One such is leprosy. In the beginning the Sisters ran the leprosy clinics in Dhapa and Titagarh, the large leprosy station in Shantinagar and the mobile clinics. Gradually, the Brothers took over the work in Titagarh and Dhapa. They also began to help the Sisters at Nirmal Hriday, the Home for the Dying. There was no special dividing line; in Titagarh the Brothers were better suited to handle the work of reconstruction in an especially hostile environment. Elsewhere longer hours were needed and the Brothers, being less regimented and enclosed, had the greater advantage.

A division of sorts applied also in the choice of overseas locations. Ten years after the Brothers were set up in India, Brother Andrew opened their first house overseas in war-ravaged Vietnam, a country where the Sisters were not working. This was not a coincidence; the choice was then made of several

OPPOSITE: MANY AIRLINES, INCLUDING AIR INDIA
AND INDIAN AIRLINES, GIVE MOTHER TERESA AND A COMPANION
SISTER FREE TRAVEL ON ANY FLIGHT.

other cities where the Sisters did not have a presence. From Skid Row in Los Angeles to a drug-infested area of Hong Kong, from crime-ridden quarters in Japan to stark poverty in Haiti, the Brothers undertook the tasks they were best at – running shelters for homeless boys, alcoholics and drug addicts.

In 1987 Brother Andrew left the order and was succeeded by Brother Geoff, also an Australian. With him came a change of gear and a time for reflection. Believing the organization to be overstretched, the total number of houses, which had gone up to 94, was brought down to 68 in 1996. Of these, 42 were in India and the remainder in 16 other countries. The number of Brothers has, over the last five years, remained almost unchanged. At the end of 1995 there were almost 450. Like the Sisters, the Brothers too are largely an Indian congregation. The 66 non-Indians are drawn from a wide range of nationalities representing every continent.

On a comparatively cool morning in March 1996, I went to 7 Mansatala Row to meet Brother Jesudas. One of the four general councillors, he was in charge during Brother Geoff's absence abroad. Aged 46, and bearded, his strong face contrasts with his gentle eyes. I was anxious to learn if Brother Geoff had brought about any significant changes in the last few years. Each man had a different imprint, explained Brother Jesudas, but the direction remained unchanged. While Brother Andrew opened houses wherever he perceived the need, there was now more emphasis on consolidation, on spiritual formation and on training. He said, 'Ours is a very hard vocation, it needs a real call to sustain it. In many ways it is harder than being a priest, for we have no position, no status. Unless we have deep faith, constantly reaffirmed by prayer, this work cannot be done. Jesus said, "Hate your life". For this we must come out of our narrow confines and our self-centredness.

Mahatma Gandhi is an inspiration for me. In everything he did, in looking after *Harijans* ["Children of God", Gandhi's name for India's "untouchables"], in cleaning their toilets, there was always the mystical presence of God.' I asked him if they converted the waifs they rescued to Catholicism. He must have had the question put to him many times before, because he replied without hesitation, 'Conversion is not our work. That is the work of God. We never ask anyone to change their religion. Our purpose is simply to try to reveal God by doing the work we do.'

As we spoke, the sound of hymns being sung resounded throughout the house. Brother Jesudas reminded me that it was a Thursday, the Brothers' weekly day off for prayer and contemplation. I asked if I could join them for a while. I was led upstairs into a room where about 20 young men sat cross-legged on the floor. Many had their eyes closed as they sang in unison. It reminded me of a scene of a *bhajan* (devotional song) group in a Hindu temple. I sat down next to a young man whom I soon learnt was well-educated and articulate, and looked as if he would have made a successful lawyer or engineer. After the singing ended, I asked Brother Jude, for that was his name, what had drawn him into such a vocation. He said that he was the first in his family to enter religious life. The urge had come to him when he was very young. After high school, he had joined a seminary in his home town. His parents were surprised but supportive. During the course of his four-year training, in the South Indian town of Nellore, he had an opportunity to see the work of the Missionaries of Charity Sisters in a house for the dying that they ran there. It touched him so deeply that he sought and obtained permission to spend a month with the Brothers who ran a leprosy home close by. In that month, all his doubts vanished. He decided not to become a priest but instead to join Mother Teresa. He was now the general treasurer but his heart lay in his work, which involved helping mentally handicapped boys in a centre near Calcutta. Did he have any regrets, I asked. He nodded and said, 'My only regret is that when I work with these kids, many of whom have suffered so much deprivation, I sometimes wish I could have trained more so that I could be more useful.'

Before I left, I asked him a question unconnected with his work. According to the constitutions, the General Chapter would be convened in October 1996 and might possibly elect a successor to Mother Teresa. If this happened, what impact would it have on the society? He thought for a few seconds before he said, 'Let us walk in Mother Teresa's footsteps. If we can be faithful to her charisma, if we continue to work with the poorest of the poor, God will never abandon us.'

A Sister with a toddler, Shishu Bhawan, Calcutta.

CHAPTER FOUR

Kalighat: The Home for the Dying

THE GREAT FAMINE in 1942–3 and the partition riots exacted an unacceptably high toll on the people of Calcutta. For thousands of families the only home they knew was its pavements. The more fortunate ones managed to build shacks of waste material in the slums that mushroomed overnight. Most simply lay down wherever they could find a place. Their days were spent eking out a living as porters or, if they were luckier, rickshaw pullers; the women and children begged outside temples and at traffic crossings. Malnourishment led to illness. Disease was rampant. Hospitals were few and overcrowded and preferred the sick, whom they felt they had a chance to save, to the dying, whom they knew they could not.

It was one such bundle of rags whom Mother Teresa had stumbled across soon after her work began at Creek Lane. Lying in a drain, her face half-eaten by rats and ants, lay a middle-aged woman. They were not far from the Campbell Hospital so, lifting her, Mother Teresa and Sister Agnes carried her there. The hospital, not having an unoccupied bed, refused to accept her. Mother Teresa, however, refused to budge and, because she insisted so firmly, the hospital gave in. They gave the woman a mattress on the floor. A few hours later she was dead. 'It was then that I decided to find a place for the dying and take care of them myself,' said Mother Teresa. Her underlying belief was that she needed a place where the poor could die with dignity.

Her search led her to Calcutta's chief medical officer. Dr Ahmed, a Muslim, recognized that this earnest middle-aged nun was offering to perform a function that essentially belonged to the Government. Obviously it was not in anyone's interest that the poor continue to die on public roads, so he showed Mother Teresa an abandoned rest house. Constructed by a Hindu benefactor for pilgrims to lodge in overnight, it stood adjacent to the city's most famous temple, the one dedicated to the goddess of destruction, Kali.

Legend has it that the right toe of the goddess Kali fell from the heavens at this particular spot and a temple was erected to sanctify it. Built along the *ghat* (bank) of a tributary of the River Ganges, itself the object of veneration, the village that grew around it came to be called Kalighat, which, was gradually anglicized into Calcutta. Then, as now, hundreds of worshippers thronged the temple, some to fulfil a vow, others to seek a cure for diseases. They come for ceremonies associated with life's journey: the naming ceremony of infants, initiation rites for adolescents, marriages and, finally, cremations on the burning *ghats* near the temple. The temple opens onto a narrow lane that is crowded with small shops selling many items needed for worship. Here, worshippers jostle with mendicants in saffron, beggars hold out tin cups, and pedestrians and shoppers go about their daily business, adding to the verve and confusion of a Calcutta bazaar.

No sooner had Mother Teresa put up the board that proclaimed the house to be Nirmal Hriday – Home for Dying Destitutes – than there was an

'For me, that is the greatest development of human life, to die in peace and in dignity, for that is for eternity.'

MOTHER TERESA TO NAVIN CHAWLA

When Mother Teresa noticed the officials, she offered to show them the work. The police officer had tears in his eyes. He said, 'There is no need, Mother.' Turning to the crowd outside he said, 'Yes, I will send this woman away, but only after you have persuaded your mothers and sisters to come here to do the work she is doing. This woman is a saint.'

Discontent, however, continued to simmer. Groups of people would frequently shout outside the entrance. One day a strange incident brought opposition to an end. A young temple priest, not quite 30, began to vomit blood. Diagnosed as an advanced case of tuberculosis, he went from hospital to hospital but none would admit him. Sick in body and heart, he was finally brought to Nirmal Hriday. There Mother Teresa herself nursed him. Gradually his rage and humiliation gave way to calm acceptance. By the time he died he was at peace. The temple priests observed the devotion with which he was treated, and noted, too, that far from being given a Christian burial, he was cremated according to the rites of his own religion.

uproar. Orthodox Hindus were affronted that Christian missionaries had moved into the temple precincts. Rumours began to circulate. She was there to convert, said some. The dead were being ministered the last rites by the Sisters and buried as Christians, said others. People took their complaints to the municipality and the police. Dr Ahmed and Calcutta's police commissioner went to Kalighat to find out for themselves. As they entered Nirmal Hriday, they saw Mother Teresa hunched over a figure whose face was a large gaping wound. With the help of a pair of tweezers she was pulling out maggots from the raw flesh. The stench was unbearable. They heard her say to the patient, 'You say a prayer in your religion, and I will say a prayer as I know it. Together we will say this prayer and it will be something beautiful for God.'

The people of Calcutta soon came to realize three things. The first was that the Missionaries of Charity were fulfilling a need. There were many religious and social organizations of all sizes and denominations in and around Calcutta that aided the poor and ailing. Yet there were very few prepared to take in those destitutes who had neither home nor hospital to die in. When they were admitted they received not only medical attention from the Sisters, among whom were invariably one or more doctors, but also love from total strangers. Second, the last rites were performed according to the deceased's faith. If patients were brought in unconscious, and were therefore unable to disclose this, a simple method was, and is, followed. Muslim males could be identified from their circumcisions, and the local *anjuman* (Muslim charitable society) was contacted to collect their bodies for Muslim burial. Sometimes a tattoo or identification mark helped reveal their faith. All other bodies were, and continue to be, cremated by Hindu rites. It would be a sacrilege for Mother Teresa to give a body a Christian burial unless specifically indicated or requested. The third factor, which people gradually grew to acknowledge, was that the Sisters, while better fed and cleanly clothed, were actually as poor as those who came through the doors.

Although the door to Nirmal Hriday is always open, a stranger, entering, feels intrusive. It takes a few minutes for the senses to adjust to the suffused quiet and orderliness. The hall has, on the left, three rows of low iron beds, two rows of which are on raised platforms. This is the men's ward and every bed is occupied. Behind each bed is a number painted on the wall. Beside many beds hang bottles of various fluids, connected intravenously to pitifully thin limbs. The quiet is broken only by the rustle of the Sisters' saris or the administering of some treatment. On several beds lie gaunt faces, each set of eyes testimony to the unrelenting harshness of their lives. When I was there I watched awkwardly as a grey-haired man on a stretcher was brought in and propped against the entrance wall. A Sister rapidly went to him and found that he had a high fever. She diagnosed malaria and put him down for a blood test. Where he lay, a shaft of light streamed in from the skylight above, directly onto his face. At first glance he seemed to be a man of about 70, but as I looked carefully at his face I realized that he was probably half that age, but old before his time.

Despite the fact that the ward was not large, the more serious cases, such as the man with malaria, were placed near the platform where the Sisters had their work tables, so that they could be more closely monitored. This also served as a small reception area and divided the men's from the women's

ward. There was a marked absence of religious decoration, but I noticed a board that proclaimed Kalighat to be 'Mother's first love'. The women's ward was slightly larger than the men's. Again, the more serious cases lay closer to where the Sisters sat. A handful of mentally disturbed women lay at the far end. Half a dozen Sisters were helped by Brothers of the order, who performed the heavier tasks. Lending them a hand were about a dozen overseas volunteers, some of whom had come to Calcutta especially to be of help while others, travelling in India, had been inspired to spend a few weeks or months helping out. Some were sponging and cleaning the patients; one said he was a doctor and was administering a penicillin injection, another was mopping the floor with a strong-smelling antiseptic, and a young man from Japan was washing linen and blankets. Among the volunteers was a Calcutta student who was fixing the electric fuses.

From 22 August 1952, the day that Mother Teresa opened the doors of Nirmal Hriday, there is an exact record of the number of cases admitted with their relevant details. A register lists the names of patients admitted, their age and address and whether they have been discharged or have died. In some cases, where people have been brought in unconscious, there is only the barest information, such as 'Female, Ripon Street'. I scrutinized the registers from the earliest years. While the 1960s and 1970s saw a mortality rate of almost 50 per cent, the 1980s witnessed a sharp drop in deaths until, by the early 1990s, the number of those who died had fallen to 10 per cent. This fall in mortality owed itself principally to improved hygiene and nutritional levels of the population at large. Many more public and charitable hospitals had been set up. Mother Teresa, for her part, had made practical linkages with several of them. This included free admission and free diagnostic treatment.

There are some who have asked why Mother Teresa has not herself established a first-class hospital in Calcutta. It needs to be explained that her mission to look after the destitute, whom Government, state or local authority is unable to assist, has remained unchanged from the very start. Her work continues to lie essentially in the streets and the slums. The buildings she has opened are still only adjuncts to the main task. Her endeavours are for the poorest of the poor, not for the middle class or the wealthy. Nor, I believe, would she want to set up a hospital, which would inevitably keep dozens of her Sisters from their street work, looking after those not necessarily belonging to her chosen constituency but whom she would, nevertheless, be unable to refuse. And where would she stop? A hospital in Calcutta is good only for Calcutta, not for Bombay, or Bogota or Bucharest. Moreover, anyone familiar with the running of large hospitals, with their scores of administrative and trade union problems, would realize that this would divert Mother Teresa from the purpose of her mission to which she has remained faithful throughout. Sister Andrea was to say, 'Hospitals are there, so there's always the possibility of people going there. But who is there for those falling beside the way, left behind on the roadside? Somebody has to be there for them.'

Meanwhile, the Sisters continue to scour the city for the sick and those in desperate need. They try to distinguish between 'street cases', the destitute and abandoned, and 'family cases', where families are unable or unwilling to care for their members. When a family case is discharged from Kalighat, the Sisters do their best to reunite him or her with their family; if they are unable to, such a patient is transferred to Prem Dan, a home for the elderly destitute. The number of beds in Kalighat is limited. On some days they get an extra 20 admissions. Their rule is to take in those whom hospitals have

AN EARLY PORTRAIT OF MOTHER TERESA IN KALIGHAT.
A SIMPLE BOARD LISTS THE NUMBER OF INMATES ON THAT DAY.

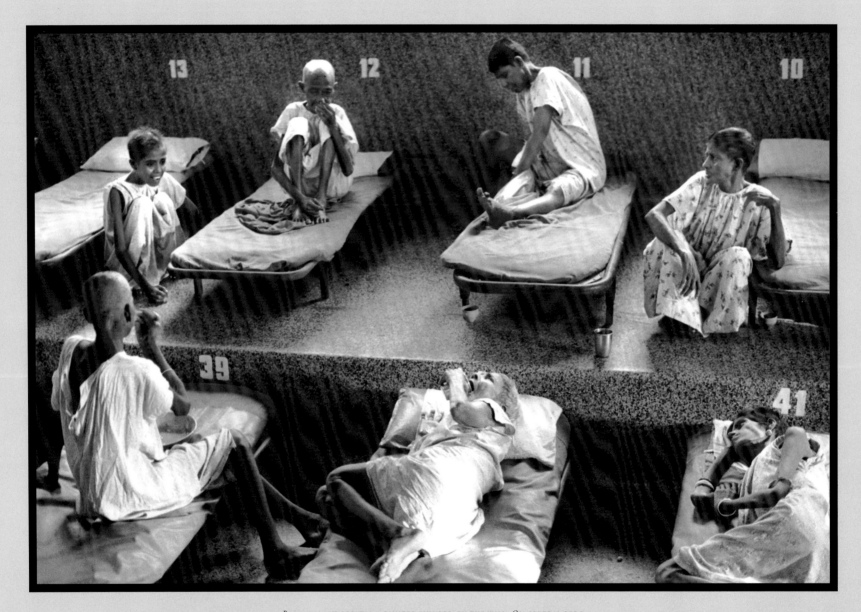

BEHIND EACH BED WAS A PAINTED NUMBER ON THE WALL. ON SEVERAL BEDS

LAY GAUNT FACES, EACH SET OF EYES TESTIMONY TO THE UNRELENTING

HARSHNESS OF THEIR LIVES.

refused; the police and municipality are encouraged to bring them cases as a matter of last resort. But I know from experience that the Sisters never refuse the abject poor. One Sister said, 'They [the poor] often come here and say, "I have fallen ill. I have nowhere to lie down. The market is so crowded. Could you not keep me for a few days?" '

Despite the inherent difficulties, every Missionaries of Charity Sister or novice must be prepared to work in Kalighat. The irony is that most of them actually plead to be sent there. It is quite evident that they need to be sturdy, for to be doctor, nurse, porter and attendant all rolled into one, six days a week, and usually well beyond their normal working hours, is back-breaking work. In addition to the physical aspect, they are constantly being called upon to listen to a request, hear a complaint or say a prayer. I have asked the Sisters in Kalighat how they look serene, even happy, working with inmates who are themselves products of the deepest adversity, and some of them close to death. How do they prepare those whom they cannot save? One Sister said, 'We tell them that they are going to face God. Every person has an origin in God, and in every human being God dwells. For me, my God is Jesus. For a Hindu, he may be Shiva or Vishnu or Brahma; for a Muslim, Allah. If a person lies unconscious, I always request another person, perhaps a Sister or a Brother or a volunteer, to sit next to the dying person and hold his or her hand, to ask pardon for the sins he or she had committed, or make an act of love or faith for God. Sometimes when this is whispered in the ear of those near death, tears roll down their cheeks. Most people you see here are not afraid of death. When I prepare someone whom I feel we have not been able to save, he often says, "That is what I came here for." '

Once, when I questioned Mother Teresa about the changes that her work had brought to the people of Calcutta, she said, 'We have come a long way. The people of Calcutta have come to know and love the poor. No one is left to die on the road. Someone, somewhere, will pick up the man and take him to us. I have seen children pick up and take old people from the street to Kalighat. People of all faiths come to share in the work. They say, "Mother Teresa, we want to help." They are willing to touch the poor, no? That's the beauty of the work. It is the same everywhere.'

One evening, as the soft shafts of light of the dying sun streamed into Kalighat, Mother Teresa said to me, 'Over the years we have rescued thousands of people from the streets, many of whom have died a beautiful death.' 'How could death be beautiful?' I asked. 'Naturally we feel lonely without a loved one,' she said. Then she added softly, 'Those who die with us, die in peace. For me that is the greatest development of human life, to die in peace and in dignity, for that is for eternity.'

As she moved through the halls talking to a patient here, inspecting a treatment there, reaching out to every extended hand, I asked her if there was any particularly poignant moment that she would never forget. She paused by the bed of a mentally retarded woman and, as she stroked her brow, she said, 'One day I picked up a man from an open drain. His body was full of sores and there were maggots crawling out of his wounds. I pulled them out, one by one. I cleaned him and bathed him myself. I tended to his sores. I knew the end was near. All the while there was no fear in his eyes. He made no complaint. As I held him in my arms, he said to me with a smile, "I have lived all my life like an animal in the street but I am going to die like an angel, loved and cared for." I gave him a special blessing so that he could see the face of God for all eternity.'

CHAPTER FIVE

Shantinagar: The Abode of Peace

Each week, at an appointed hour, a mobile dispensary comes to a halt by the main gate of the Loreto Convent at Entally. A folding table and two collapsible chairs are quickly taken from the van and placed on the pavement at the head of a queue of almost 50 men, women and children. Sister Collett, accompanied by two novices, jumps out and opens up a register that she carries with her. I notice that it has almost a thousand names. 'Shanti,' she calls out, and a young woman, not quite 30, steps forward. Shanti is slim and attractive. She wears a gold bangle on her right hand. Below the bangle her hand is bandaged. I notice that Shanti has no fingers; all that remains is a stump. Shanti has leprosy. Sister Collett asks her some questions in Bengali. Slowly the girl answers. Yes, she did take the drugs given to her last week quite regularly. No, there has been no fresh ulceration. Her hand is inspected, then rebandaged. She accepts her weekly free dose of an expensive medicine and moves away.

Swapun is next. Clearly he has not been as lucky as Shanti, for he has a bulbous face and the tissues on his nose have been eaten away by the disease. Fortyish, he neglected the early signs when treatment could have completely cured him. Instead he hid his tell-tale patches until deformity set in. When he was finally unable to conceal this, he lost his job at the factory, where he earned a good wage. For months he hunted for another job, but the evident signs of leprosy closed all doors. In the end, his family told him that no one

would marry his only daughter if they knew that she had a leper for a father. One night he stole out of his home, never to return. Sick at heart, he found his way to a *bustee* inhabited entirely by the leprosy-afflicted. From them he learned about Mother Teresa and her street clinics. For four weeks now he has been on therapy. The Sisters have advised him to attend regularly, as this is the key to a cure. He attends regularly, not only because he is desperate to get better but also because the medicines are accompanied by a much-needed packet of rice each week.

The mobile dispensaries, which make a number of regular halts as they meander through Calcutta's streets, were themselves the outcome of the closure, in the mid-1950s, of a leprosy hospital in Calcutta. Mother Teresa petitioned hard to keep the Gobra Hospital going, for thousands of cases were registered there. Any change could cause a great deal of dislocation. But pressure from developers and local residents, who had wanted it moved out of their midst, prevailed. Realizing that it was very difficult for the poor to reach the new location on the outskirts of the city, Mother Teresa hunted for a suitable site to set up a clinic of her own. In the end she managed to find a site almost as centrally situated as the hospital. However, the residents of the new location were soon up in arms at the prospect of a leprosy clinic in their neighbourhood. One morning when Mother Teresa went to inspect the site she was confronted by the local councillor at the head of a crowd of residents.

No sooner did she alight from the van than she was greeted by a barrage of stones. Her response, as ever, was practical. 'I don't think God wants us to open a clinic here,' she said. 'Let us pray and find out what He does want.'

Inspiration came in the form of an ambulance donated by American benefactors. Mother Teresa immediately decided to convert this into the first of her mobile leprosy clinics. Knowing that it was difficult for the poor to leave their begging stations, she decided instead to go to them. At that very time, Doctor Sen, a renowned Bengali skin and leprosy specialist, retired from his long innings at a Government hospital. Not knowing how he would spend his time, he offered his honorary services to Mother Teresa, who accepted with alacrity. The first mobile leprosy clinic was launched by Archbishop Perier in September 1957. From a single van, the service eventually grew until today a chain of ambulatory stations provides treatment to hundreds of thousands of patients, not merely in Calcutta, but in cities all over Asia and Africa.

From biblical times until comparatively recently there was no effective cure for this disease, with its horrendous disfigurement and social rejection. While, inexplicably, leprosy vanished from Europe in the 16th century, 12 million cases still exist in Asia, Africa, South America and the Middle East. A new treatment in the form of the multi-drug regimen, introduced in most of these countries from the early 1980s, effectively brought many millions of cases under control. The 1960s and the 1970s, however, presented a far bleaker picture, for many Asian and African programmes lacked committed funds and technical personnel. The leprosy-afflicted came to fill a special place in Mother Teresa's world of destitutes and she rapidly set up leprosaria, clinics, rehabilitation and surgical units as well as mobile stations, wherever the disease was particularly widespread.

Unlike most other diseases, a complete cure in leprosy does not necessarily lessen the stigma and social boycott, as I was soon to discover. In the Seemapuri home in Delhi, I met a young man and his mother. She was in her early forties. The disease had eaten her face; in place of her nose there was a gaping hole. Before the development of the disease, they lived in a remote mountain village in North India. Her first inkling that something was wrong came when she began to lose sensation in her right hand. She had pricked her finger and it had bled, but she had felt no pain. Gradually she had lost sensation in both hands.

Terrified, she prayed in the temple. From temples to soothsayers in distant towns, who sold her magic potions, she went to them all. When large patches began to appear on her face, the disease could no longer be concealed. The word spread like wildfire in the village, and the village council was convened. It decided that the only way of saving the rest of the community, including her own family members, was for her to be banished.

While her husband stayed behind with the other children, the eldest son, unable to bear the parting with his mother, accompanied her. They wandered from city to town, clinic to hospital. When their meagre savings ran out, they slept in alleyways and begged for food in temples. Finally, when she was on the verge of suicide, they reached Delhi. Here, a kindly leprosy beggar extended a helping hand and led them to Seemapuri, where the Sisters welcomed them. They helped the son get a job in the city, and they eventually cured her of the disease.

Her scars inside, however, were too deep to heal. Today she helps the Sisters with their washing and cleaning; for her this is, and always will be, her refuge.

Mother Teresa had often spoken to me about the Gandhiji Prem Niwas (abode of love) Leprosy Centre at Titagarh, a small town about an hour's drive from Calcutta. Mother Teresa named it after Mahatma Gandhi (the suffix *-ji* being an honorific expressing respect in India), the messiah of India's freedom struggle, who championed the cause of India's downtrodden, including the country's four million leprosy-afflicted. Titagarh's outpatients' hall, where I awaited its director, Brother Mariadas, displayed a pencil sketch of Gandhiji nursing two leprosy sufferers. The centre was the outcome of persistent requests to Mother Teresa by the leprosy-afflicted of Titagarh to set up a clinic in their midst, as they found it difficult and expensive to travel to Calcutta for treatment. They persuaded Mother Teresa to visit their settlement. Here she found a pitiable situation: rampant disease affected dozens of families, who had been pushed out of town to the edge of a swamp alongside the railway tracks. There was no drinking water, no drainage, no sewage facilities and no electricity. Crime and violence were endemic. There was virtually no medical care available to them. Seeing their immediate need, Mother Teresa started sending her Sisters each week, but soon realized Titagarh would need a full-time clinic. Two Brothers, Christo Das and his young assistant Mariadas, were put in charge to establish one.

Piecemeal measures, the Brothers soon found, would not help. Overcoming the initial resistance from the gangs that infested the *bustee*, they organized an enthusiastic workforce of men, women and even children, to fill in the swamps and gradually construct small self-contained cottages: two

WAITING TO MEET MOTHER TERESA.

small rooms, a kitchen and a toilet. No longer in hovels, the lepers experienced for the first time a wholly different quality of life. It pitched them into renewed effort. In time a whole complex was built up before their eyes: a rehabilitation centre, a hospital, even a cafeteria. The buildings stretched along the railway line, until it became a long and narrow complex, a mile from one end to the other. Mother Teresa petitioned the municipality for water, drainage and electricity. Children were put into local schools. Men and women were persuaded to give up illicit distillation of liquor and helped to set up small shops and stalls of their own. All this time the attack on disease continued apace. Ten years after it all began in 1958, a social transformation had been effected.

Brother Mariadas led me on a tour. The strong smell of antiseptic announced the hospital from afar. It was proof of its efficacy that there were no longer any local patients. Some were from as far away as the neighbouring states of Orissa, Bihar and Assam. Hospitalization was completely free and those who needed prosthetic equipment were helped to obtain it. Near the hospital stood the houses, which reminded me of the model villages I had seen in many parts of the developing world. As we approached, little children ran out to greet Brother Mariadas well before he had seen them. It was the rehabilitation centre, to which Brother Mariadas finally took me, which was the focal point. It was a long and narrow hall in which stood dozens of looms. On these sat leprosy patients weaving hundreds of saris to be worn by the Missionaries of Charity. Their annual production was about 4,000, to be sent from here to every centre of the Missionaries of Charity around the world. Many of the leprosy-afflicted had incomplete hands and it seemed amazing that they could engage in any meaningful activity. But they were hard at work,

their quiet dignity a testimony to their conquest of hardship and disease.

By contrast, the crowd that surrounded Mother Teresa at Seemapuri on a hot summer afternoon in 1993 was angry and resentful. They were full of complaints, which they hurled at her in rapid succession. Was Mother Teresa aware how bad the *dal* (souped lentils, a staple ingredient of the diet) tasted? She would never be able to eat it herself, said one. But she had just had it for lunch, and it was fine, she replied. Don't eat it again, he retorted, or you'll fall ill. We are not allowed to smoke in the dormitories, objected another. Try not to smoke at all, said Mother with a smile, or, if you must, step onto the verandah. Look at my hand, said a third, it's been bleeding and the Sisters have not done anything about it. We'll show it to the doctor in a little while, replied Mother Teresa, and the man lapsed into a somewhat satisfied silence. Look at my shoes, remonstrated another, the rehabilitation unit has made them so badly that they hurt. We'll get them to fit you into another pair, she said. It continued in this vein for another 20 minutes or so, until everyone seemed to have had their say. To each she replied calmly and gently. Finally, silence descended. As she prepared to move away, they rose and, one by one, came to touch her feet. She restrained as many as she could, for she doesn't encourage this practice and invariably tries to pre-empt it by folding her hands into a *namaste*. It is, however, a battle she invariably loses, for in India this is a custom that signifies respect for an elder, and is a daily, commonplace occurrence. As they turned away, Mother Teresa said to me, 'Each of them has suffered so much pain and humiliation. Once in a while their bitterness overcomes them. Sometimes the Sisters have a very difficult time calming them. Yet when we ask our young Sisters who would like to go and work with the lepers, every hand is up.'

It was soon the Sisters' turn to have Mother Teresa to themselves, even if it was only for a short while. Although work brought Mother Teresa to Delhi several times a year, she was not able to visit all her Delhi houses each time. Seemapuri's turn had come after some months. As I watched the Sisters crowding around her, giggling or touching her hem, they seemed like little children. It was a scene reminiscent of the return of a real mother or a well-loved friend.

When Mother Teresa spoke to me about the anger of the leprosy-afflicted, particularly those who were scarred for life, I was reminded of an incident that had occurred a few years before, 1,000 miles away in Shantinagar in West Bengal. During my visit there, as I had stood talking to Sister Albert, the superior, the morning's calm was suddenly shattered. A man, shouting loudly and waving a stick, menacingly bore down on us. I had been quite startled, but Sister Albert had retained her composure. When the man was a few feet away from us he had stopped short. Sister Albert had spoken to him, and he had thrown down the

'I love the people of Calcutta. They have a warmth which you don't see anywhere else.'

MOTHER TERESA TO NOTED INDIAN AUTHOR KHUSHWANT SINGH

stick and walked away. She explained to me that Pramod, for that was his name, had not recovered from the desertion of his wife when she learned he had leprosy. She had left him for another man, abandoning her children in the process.

But not all cases had such unhappy endings. Shantinagar, according to Sister Albert, was a 'miracle'. In the Sisters' vocabulary, miracles happen several times a day when things go perfectly, and there was, indeed, much about Shantinagar that reflected its success. Soon after Titagarh had been developed, Mother Teresa realized the inestimable benefit of a leprosy treatment and rehabilitation centre in the coal-mining areas bordering the neighbouring state of Bihar, where the disease was widespread and medical treatment scant. She persuaded, without too much difficulty it seems, the chief minister of West Bengal to lease her a large tract of land on a token payment of one rupee a year. But to turn the 34 acres of scrub into a leprosy settlement needed funds, which just then were scarce.

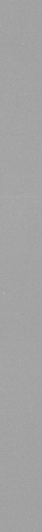

*'Every child is
precious, every child is
a gift of God.'*
MOTHER TERESA

Mother Teresa has often said that money has never posed a problem. She has only needed to pray. Her prayers were answered when Pope Paul VI, after the conclusion of his tour of India, donated to Mother Teresa the limousine that had been specially flown in for his use, in turn a gift from the American people. Mother Teresa would have been an unlikely occupant of such a car, though she might have converted the limousine into an ambulance! So she decided to sell it but, instead of a straight sale, she devised a raffle, which raised far more money than would otherwise have been expected, such was the publicity that the event attracted. I asked her how she had got the idea. In a tone that spoke volumes, she replied, 'If you learn to pray, you too will get these ideas.'

Money was now in hand, but the more difficult part was about to begin. In 1968, Mother Teresa sent Sister Francis Xavier, a Yugoslav nun, to tame the wilderness. She started, as the Sisters always do, by planting fruit trees, which included a whole orchard of mango and lime. Land was levelled for rice and wheat; a pond was enlarged and stocked with fish, a free supply of protein for the malnourished. Then began the construction work: cottages for the patients, a hospital, a large rehabilitation centre, a crèche. The first arrivals were taught to make bricks and then to build their own houses, according to simple designs given to them. A Shishu Bhawan was built to segregate healthy children from their infectious parents. Doctors from nearby Asansol volunteered their services and attended the hospital to handle the more serious patients and to perform surgery. Gradually, the residents of Shantinagar became a largely self-sufficient community, who grew most of their own food and engaged in simple crafts, including the weaving of baskets, which they sold in nearby towns.

Their workshop produced special shoes for the many who needed them; even the soft rubber from used car tyres went to line the insides. Animal waste was converted into an odourless gas that was piped into the kitchens. Hundreds of coconut and teak trees were planted; the former a source of nutrients, and the latter for much-needed timber for these and other developments. Everywhere the patients, even those with deformity, were involved in community work. Meanwhile, the children and youths, who were housed in separate dormitories, attended local schools and some even had computer studies as part of their education.

Some years ago Mother Teresa offered a gathering of dignitaries, senior civil servants and diplomats in New Delhi a tiny glimpse of the revolution that the Missionaries of Charity had brought about when she said, 'Governments have been very good to me everywhere, in the Middle East, in Africa and in India… in giving me land to rehabilitate them [the leprosy-afflicted]. We tried to get whole families together. In some places we buy building materials so that they can build their own houses. We pay them to build them.

'They have their own shops, their own little schools and their land, so they feel they are somebody. I think this is the greatest cure, to make them feel that they, too, are chosen ones. Many of the children [of our leprosy patients] have now grown up, some are studying, they are working, they are married and have settled down in life, without a sign of the disease. A new energy has come into their lives.'

I ONCE ASKED MOTHER TERESA WHAT SHE EXPECTED OF HER SISTERS. SHE REPLIED, 'LET GOD RADIATE AND LIVE HIS LIFE IN HER AND THROUGH HER IN THE SLUMS. LET THE SICK AND SUFFERING FIND IN HER A REAL ANGEL OF COMFORT AND CONSOLATION.'

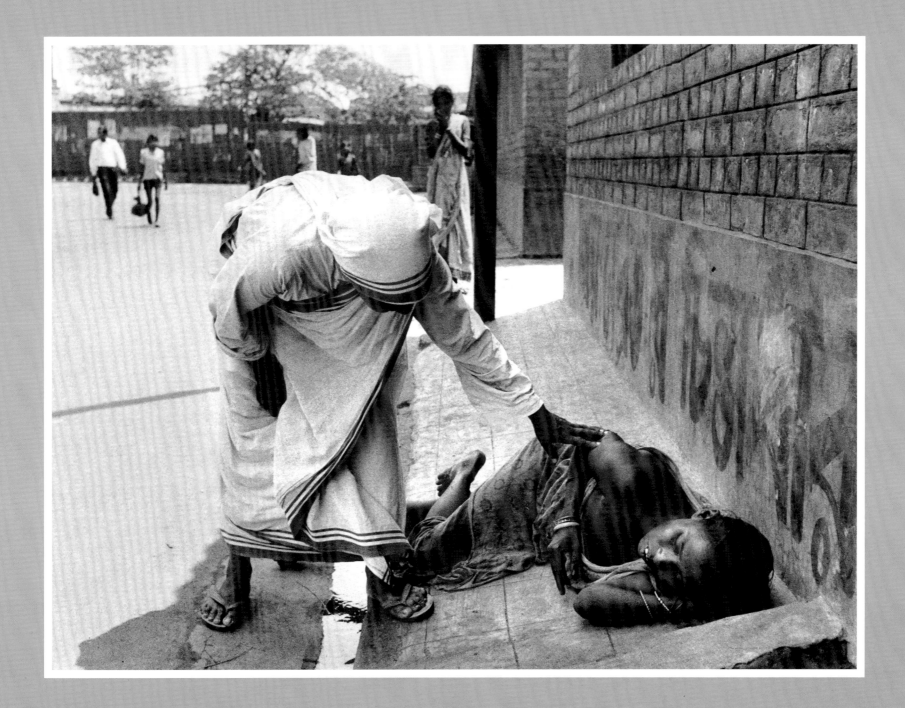

CHAPTER SIX

Shishu Bhawan: A Home for Children

GITA WAS A child who had forgotten how to smile. I did not at first notice her. The cheerful crèche that I had entered in Shantinagar was alive with activity and noise. A dozen three- and four-year-olds were playing with toys or tumbling on the floor. Almost as many toddlers were standing in their cribs. A Sister held in her arms a wailing infant, whom she wasn't succeeding in quieting. 'See, children, who has come to see you. Say good morning now,' said Sister Albert. This was followed by a loud chorus of 'Good morning, uncle'. A lively four-year-old hurled his sports car at me, which fortunately missed. 'Naughty boy, naughty boy,' clucked Sister Albert. A little girl of three tugged repeatedly at my clothes until she was sure of my undivided attention. Gradually my eyes came to rest on a girl who seemed too big for a crib. Without being able to define it at first, I sensed there was something different about her. The realization came slowly. During the ten minutes that I had been there, unlike the other children, she did not once turn to look at the stranger who had entered their midst. Instead she stood steadfastly facing the wall.

Sister Albert explained why. Two years before there had been a terrible fire in the neighbouring town of Dumka. Several houses had burned to the ground and many lives were lost. One of those miraculously rescued was a wailing infant who was rushed, barely alive, to the hospital. For weeks she hovered between life and death. In the end she survived, but her body was a mass of scars. During the many months in the hospital no relative came to claim her. The hospital staff tried hard to locate her parents or even a distant kinsman. Finally, no longer able to keep the child, they brought her to the Missionaries of Charity in Shantinagar. They were aware that, although a leprosy institution, it had a Shishu Bhawan and a crèche where healthy children were separated from their infectious parents. Sister Albert took in the child. Further operations were required, first to enable her to open her mouth more fully, then to enable her to use her fingers better. But if she were ever to look like a normal child, she would need extensive plastic surgery. This the doctors were willing to perform free of charge, but Sister Albert explained that the child was too traumatized to bear any further pain for some considerable time. The Sisters gave the little child the name of Gita.

All the while that Sister Albert spoke about her, Gita continued to face the wall. It was only when the Sister called her name persistently that she turned round briefly. Her face was completely impassive. She never once smiled. At the age of three, Gita was consumed by an anguish far deeper than she could bear.

If infants were not abandoned in streets or on doorsteps, or left unwanted in hospitals and clinics, there would, I expect, have been no need for Mother Teresa to start her Shishu Bhawans. Perhaps that explains why, alone of Mother Teresa's institutions, they are such cheerful places, with brightly painted walls and chintzy curtains and lots of toys, donations that Mother Teresa readily accepts. The story of each child would reveal its share of sorrow, but Mother Teresa and her Sisters do their best to provide the children with love and care, nutrition and medical attention and, wherever possible, a set of parents to adopt them.

The Shishu Bhawans are usually located close to the Sisters' convents, for premature and sick children are provided with constant attention. The numbers of children vary from 20 to 200, depending on the shape and size of the building. Buildings themselves differ greatly, from a second Shishu Bhawan in Delhi (constructed and gifted especially to Mother Teresa by a local industrialist) to a large rambling colonial house in Calcutta, which Mother Teresa herself bought many years ago, a few hundred yards down the road from Motherhouse. In the latter, at any given time, there are as many as 200 infants, some of them premature babies battling for their lives in incubators. These are usually unwanted children collected from clinics and nursing homes. Additionally, Sisters, novices and volunteers look after about a 100 children aged up to about seven or eight. There is a kindergarten school for the younger children, while the older ones are sent to the nearest regular school with all costs met by the Missionaries of Charity.

'Some weeks back, at midnight, I heard a child's
cry at our gate. When I went down, I saw this little one. I
don't think she was more than seven. Crying, she said, "I
went to my father and my father did not want me,"
and she crossed the road and went to her mother
and her mother did not want her.
"But you want me," she said.'

The leprosy centres almost invariably have a small Shishu Bhawan so that the new-born can be insulated from infectious parents soon after birth. Children of leprosy patients are invariably born free of the disease, but constant kissing and fondling can communicate it. The parents can visit as often as they wish, but in the initial periods are discouraged from too close a contact. 'One day,' said Mother Teresa, 'a couple brought their new-born child to me. They put the baby between them and each looked at the little one, their hands going to the child, wanting to kiss the child and falling back again. I can never forget their deep love.'

SHISHU BHAWAN, CALCUTTA.

'I have never refused a child. Never. Not one,' said Mother Teresa almost fiercely. 'Each child is precious. Each is created by God.' After she opened the first Shishu Bhawan in Calcutta, letters were sent to all clinics and nursing homes asking them to inform the Missionaries of Charity of any unwanted children, even handicapped, physically or mentally, or premature. Today the Sisters in Shishu Bhawans in cities all over the world ask only that they be telephoned; they are willing themselves to collect the child. Wherever possible, destitute pregnant women are given temporary refuge until childbirth. After the baby is born, if the mother cannot be persuaded to keep it or her circumstances do not permit, the Sisters take the child. This is invariably a matter of last resort. 'I cannot give the love a real mother can give,' says Mother Teresa. 'But a child is a gift of God. The miracle is that every day many families, and in India mainly Hindu families, come and adopt our children. Thousands and thousands have gone to such loving homes.'

Mother Teresa maintains stoutly that she is fighting abortion with adoption. She knows her views have many detractors but this doesn't bother her in the least. She has implicit faith in the Roman Catholic doctrine of birth control and abhors the word 'abortion'. In practically every visit to the United States and Europe she speaks out against it. In her Nobel lecture, which she delivered in Oslo in 1979, millions of television viewers heard her say that she believed the greatest destroyer of peace was not war but abortion.

'Many people are very concerned with the children of India, with the children of Africa where quite a number die, maybe of malnutrition, of hunger and so on, but millions are dying deliberately by the will of the mother. If a mother can kill her own child, what is left?'

She is, of course, aware that her views are not widely shared and most governments, the press and the intelligentsia do not support them. Within the Church there are many denominations that fail to agree with her, and polls in America and Europe have revealed that a majority of Catholics favour contraception and abortion under many circumstances. Her critics point out that several countries where she works are vastly over-populated, and these problems are unlikely to go away by her simply offering to take in all the unwanted children. To them Mother Teresa replies that she advocates natural family planning involving abstention by couples, and that in her many Natural Family Planning Centres, instructions are given in the rhythm method. She quotes figures for the thousands of births prevented in this manner.

Although the Shishu Bhawans are bursting at their seams, there is a steady outflow of children taken into adoption. Many of the prospective parents that I have spoken to in centres in India belong to ordinary middle-class Hindu families. When the programme started, there were more Christian families coming forward to adopt, and many more children went abroad. This trend has now reversed itself. Large numbers of Hindus now apply. Whereas in the earlier years they were fussy about wanting only good-looking boys, most of them now make a choice on their initial visit and many select girls. The children that are now sent abroad are mainly physically handicapped, for whom facilities in developing countries are very expensive and difficult to come by. Sadly, the mentally handicapped are very difficult to place but Mother Teresa runs some homes for children who would otherwise surely die on the streets. These include the Nirmala Kennedy Centre in Calcutta. In a large bungalow set in a spacious garden, scores of children play on swings and slides. Inside the scene is more sombre, for here lie spastics, paralytics, the mentally disabled and seriously physically disabled children, some with no arms or legs. It is also comparatively difficult to place normal children over seven or eight; most people want to adopt either infants or small children. Boys too old for adoption are sent to the boys' homes run by the Missionaries of Charity Brothers. Here they are educated, taught a trade and helped to find employment. Many people also help to sponsor the education of such children. Depending on their scholastic abilities, some are encouraged to study further. Girls who do not want to study beyond school are found suitable husbands. In India, where arranged marriages and dowries are still considered the norm, Mother Teresa is realistic enough to find them 'nice boys'. Local benefactors invariably queue up to give them a few gold ornaments, some saris and utensils, furniture and a little money in a bank account opened in their names. Calcutta especially is full of such families, as is evidenced by anyone visiting Motherhouse on festivals and feast days, when the courtyard and the street outside are filled with couples there to greet Mother Teresa and the Sisters. One of the jokes amongst the Sisters is that a prospective bridegroom for any of the girls had better watch out, for he is likely to inherit several mothers-in-law with his bride!

An eventual bridegroom whom I came to know as a young man was called Raj Kumar. One day a Sister from the Shishu Bhawan in Delhi rang me and asked if they could send him to see me. He was one of 'their children', brought up in a Shishu Bhawan and thereafter in a boys' home. He had taken a matriculation degree, but had not wished to study further. He had had a string of part-time jobs and, at the time, worked occasionally as a waiter at wedding banquets. Like all young men of his age, he wanted a government job. Could I help? He told me he was registered at an employment exchange but had not received a call for an interview with any prospective government agency. I told him he would have to be patient and meanwhile I could help him get a temporary job. I spoke to someone I knew who constantly needed full-time waiters in his well-known restaurant. The youth was promptly employed. A few weeks later he came to see me, looking thin and visibly drawn. I soon discovered that he had been shifted to another job outside the restaurant, which involved carrying heavy deliveries. He said it was because he had revealed that he had had leprosy and tuberculosis as a child. He was immediately ostracized and the others soon demanded of the management that he be sacked, failing which they threatened to resign *en masse*. Fortunately, a few weeks later he received a notice for an interview with a government department and, without too much fuss, was able to secure the post. A post in government may not bring much money, but it brings with it a lifetime of security. After two years it also brought a little one-roomed flat. This was beyond his wildest dreams. A few months later he came to see me with a box of traditional Indian sweetmeats. He had decided to get married to an 'alumnus' of Shishu Bhawan who now lent the Sisters a helping hand in exchange for her board and lodging. A few weeks later the Sisters and I attended a traditional Hindu wedding. Two Sisters were present to represent both sides of the family; one gave the bride away, while the other received her in her new home and family.

'I eat my fill but I must remember
those who don't have.'
MOTHER TERESA

CHAPTER SEVEN

The Final Chapter

IT WAS 20 August 1993. Mother Teresa had been invited to New Delhi to accept the Rajiv Gandhi National Sadhbhavana (peace) Award from the chairman of the award committee, the vice-president of India, in the presence of the prime minister and Mrs Sonia Gandhi, the widow of the former Indian prime minister. A thousand invitations had been issued for an event that would bring together a host of distinguished people. A few hours before the ceremony, Mother Teresa developed a high fever. A local doctor diagnosed malaria and recommended hospitalization. While a Sister was deputed to receive the award in her place, Mother Teresa herself was taken to a public hospital where she remained for over a week. The president of India made inquiries; the prime minister visited. Ambassadors called, conveying wishes of speedy recovery on behalf of their governments. The hospital switchboard was jammed with calls from all over the world. I was asked to inquire whether she preferred treatment abroad. She stoutly refused, asking time and again only that she return to her beloved Calcutta. It was ten days before the doctors agreed to discharge her. The prime minister offered a special plane to fly her back. On reaching Calcutta she waved aside the ambulance that was taken to the plane. Instead she walked to the terminal and nimbly stepped into her mission van. She was home.

During her hospitalization, I had noticed her restlessness, particularly when the doctors came calling. I was reminded of an incident which I was told had occurred in Calcutta some years earlier. In December 1989 she had fainted as she was coming down the stairs in Motherhouse. When she came to, she found herself in the intensive-care unit of a private nursing home. Believing she could ill-afford the cost, she struggled to get out of bed but found she had been wired up. 'In all conscience, doctor,' she said, 'I cannot stay here.' Upon which the doctor replied, 'In all conscience, Mother, I cannot let you go.'

A few years later, when she developed cardiac complications while visiting her house in Tijuana in Mexico, she was rushed in almost similar circumstances across the border to a Californian hospital. For days she hovered on the brink. Each hospital bulletin made front-page news across the world; millions prayed for her recovery. However, just as soon as she was better, an attending doctor told me that she tried to escape. 'Come, Sister, let us go,' she said one night to the young Sister of her order who was with her. But she had not taken the staff nurses into account: they, seeing her leave her room, bundled her back into bed, and mounted guard against any further attempt.

It was after this serious illness that I asked her whether the rapid increase in her work, both in India and overseas, was sustainable. Several houses were being opened, notably in Eastern Europe and the former Soviet Union. The concern I reflected was born out of the growing feeling that in the strength of this organization might lie its weakness, for authority seemed to be entirely concentrated in the hands of one individual. What would happen when she

'We are poor but out of choice. Otherwise how can we hope to understand our poor?'
MOTHER TERESA

passed away, I inquired? She said nothing but pointed her finger heavenwards. A few weeks later I asked again, whereupon she disarmed me by saying, 'Let me go first,' and added with a smile, 'Just as God has found me, He will find somebody else. The work is God's work and He will see to it.' I asked if she controlled everything. She shook her head briskly and said, 'No, we now have many Sisters. Every house has a superior, then a number of houses together are placed under a regional superior. Each regional superior is responsible for a province, for example Western Europe, America and so on. Then we have four councillors general. We have Church laws which direct us, rules that will guide and lead us, otherwise there will be confusion. If you go to any country where we work you will see exactly the same thing: Sisters sitting on the floor, the same poverty, the cheapest food, and so on. Mother Teresa is not in all of the houses at the same time. Yet the work goes on.' Then she added something in which, I believe, may lie the key to the endurance of their order. 'If we remain wedded to our poverty and do not end up unconsciously serving the rich, all will be well.'

From the very start, the order has been run according to the constitutions, written first in 1950 and enlarged and amended from time to time. These rules govern their daily lives, their charter of duties and, inescapably, the election to the posts of superior general and the four councillors general. The General Chapter is the congregation's final authority. It has met regularly every six years since 1967 and comprises about a hundred delegates, including all regional superiors. Elections are by secret ballot; an absolute majority is needed. Unknown to most people, who believe that Mother Teresa will remain the head of the order for her lifetime, it is elections that determine who will remain and who will be elected superior general.

'No one is (now) allowed to die on the streets.
Someone, somewhere will bring him to us.'
MOTHER TERESA

Mother Teresa first tried to step down in 1973, when she was 63 years old, and then once again in 1979. On both occasions the chapter voted her back. After her illness in 1989, she sought the Vatican's permission to convene the chapter in September 1990, a year earlier than scheduled. Once again, the Sisters resisted. Some senior Sisters wished to know whether they were specifically debarred from voting for Mother Teresa and sought Father van Exem's advice. He informed them that while Mother Teresa had made plain her intention to the Vatican, there was no bar on the Sisters voting for her if they so wished. The Sisters

MOTHER TERESA IN KALIGHAT.

overwhelmingly voted that she remain. 'I wanted to be free, but God has His own plans,' she said. 'This is His work, not mine. As long as we remain wedded to Him and our poverty, the work will prosper. I am not important.'

At the time of writing, the general chapter was due to meet again, in October 1996. Once again, there is speculation about Mother Teresa's desire to step down and whether it would be accepted by the nuns. I spoke to a senior Sister about the uncertainty. Not for a moment did she dwell on any ripple on the surface, or currents under the waters. She replied without a moment's hesitation, 'Mother has always said that God created this out of nothing and He has used nothingness, naturally meaning herself, to be able to do this work. She has often said, "I have done for God, and to God, and with God, and it is God's work. He is perfectly capable of finding someone when I am gone, somebody who is even smaller." The question of a call for this work and the work itself is all beyond each single Sister. None of us has created or done anything. Each of us serves in one place but the mastermind is God himself. We will leave it to Him.'

Mother Teresa has always held that she is only an instrument, and an imperfect one at that: a 'pencil in the hands of the Lord'. Malcolm Muggeridge wrote in *Something Beautiful for God* (Collins, London, 1971) 'It is, of course, true that the wholly dedicated like Mother Teresa do not have biographies. Biographically speaking, nothing happens to them. To live for, and in, others as she and the Sisters of the Missionaries of the Charity do, is to eliminate happenings, which are a factor of the ego and the will.

"Yet not I, but Christ liveth in me", is one of her favourite sayings.' It is this that makes for her complete humility and this, too, that causes her to treat beggar and king alike. She is, nevertheless, the inspiration that binds the whole work together. It is her example that causes the Sisters, even a continent or two away, to say, 'Mother, this' and 'Mother, that' in constant refrain, as if she were in the next room and likely to walk in at any moment. The same charisma also attracts the new entrants and keeps the flock together, with surprisingly few departures over the years.

The work, of course, but her inspiration, too, has led to her becoming one of the world's best-known people. She is certainly the most decorated. The number of countries and institutions that have heaped awards on her is so large that the Sisters have given up trying to compile a list. Mother Teresa, who accepts all recognition in the name of the poor she serves, forgets about it almost as soon as the occasion is over, anxious to get back to the 'real work'. She doesn't say so, but any money that comes along makes her eyes gleam, for there is always a school to be started, a feeding programme to be strengthened, medicines needed. On one occasion when I had accompanied her to a ceremony in New Delhi, she received a very heavy trophy, which required two men to carry it to the dais. Halfway through the proceedings, she had to leave in order to catch a flight back to Calcutta. On the way to the airport, she remembered the trophy and asked me to collect it and send it to her convent. Believing that such a large silver-plated plaque would sit rather awkwardly in the parlour of Motherhouse, I asked her where she would keep it. 'Keep it?' she exclaimed, surprised at my question. 'I'll sell it! It'll bring medicine for our patients. I'm sure the organizers won't mind.'

THESE ARE CASES THAT HOSPITALS ARE UNABLE TO ACCEPT. THE MORE SERIOUS ONES ARE PLACED NEAR THE SISTERS' WORK TABLES, WHERE THEY CAN BE CONSTANTLY MONITORED.

Her country by adoption, India, was the first to honour her when, in 1962, she received the Padma Shri (the Order of the Lotus). This was followed by the Ramon Magsaysay Award from the Philippines, also in 1962. Its timing was particularly opportune. She was anxious to start a home for children not far from the Taj Mahal in Agra. The problem was the lack of adequate funds. The Sisters got down to pray. On the very day that Mother Teresa reluctantly informed her Sisters in Agra that they would have to postpone the project there came the announcement of the prize. It carried with it a sum of 50,000 rupees, the exact amount needed to start the home.

The US $21,500 that accompanied the first International Pope John XXIII Prize (1971) came precisely when money was needed to develop Shantinagar. With the US $15,000 that came with the Joseph Kennedy Jr Foundation Award she founded a home that she had planned for the crippled, spastic and mentally retarded children in Calcutta, which she named the Nirmala Kennedy Centre. In 1972, the government of India awarded her the Jawaharlal Nehru Award for International Understanding, which also brought a large amount; this was equally usefully employed. With it came a citation that read in part, 'Someday perhaps mankind will devise satisfactory solutions for every human predicament. But as long as compassion counts for something in the human condition, the hopes of defeated men everywhere, despairing men at the end of their tether, will rest on a chosen few, for whom the giving is all. One such messenger of mercy is Mother Teresa.'

The following year, 1973, she received from Prince Philip in London the first Templeton Prize for Progress in Religion. She had been chosen from over 2,000 nominations received from 80 countries by nine judges drawn from the world's major religions. With it came a cash prize larger even than the Nobel Prize. Four years later, Prince Philip, this time as chancellor of Cambridge University, conferred on her the university's honorary degree of divinity. He remarked in his speech that 'the Reverend Mother, whom we are delighted to see among us, would reply, if you inquired about her career, that it was of no importance.' The assembly broke into cheers.

In retrospect, it seems natural that Mother Teresa should have received the Nobel Prize for Peace. When news reached her that the Norwegian Nobel Committee had named her, her first reaction was 'I am unworthy' and she sent word to the organizers that as she was only a symbol, she would accept the award 'in the name of the poor', which the committee accepted. The selection of Mother Teresa was to many an assurance that politics was not the only way to pursue peace. She travelled to Oslo, fittingly accompanied by her first two postulants, Sisters Agnes and Gertrude. Her arrival on a cold day in December 1979 to relentless media attention caused her to remark later that facing the press was harder than bathing a leper. On 10 December, in the presence of the King of Norway and a glittering gathering, a simple woman, wearing a sari that cost about a dollar, received the ultimate accolade.

The chairman of the Norwegian Nobel Committee, Professor John Sannes, chose his words with great care when he said, 'The hallmark of her work has been respect for the individual and the individual's worth and dignity. The lowliest and most wretched, the dying destitutes, the abandoned lepers, have been received by her and her Sisters with warm compassion devoid of condescension, based on this reverence for Christ in Man… In her eyes the person who, in the accepted sense, is the recipient is also the giver and the one who gives the most. Giving – giving something of oneself – is what confers real joy, and the person who is allowed to give is the one who receives the most precious gift. Where others see clients or customers, she sees fellow workers, a relationship based not on expectation of gratitude on the one part but on mutual understanding and respect, and a warm human and enriching contact... This is the life of Mother Teresa and her Sisters – a life of strict poverty and long days and nights of toil, a life that affords little room for other joys but the most precious.'

What captured almost as much attention as the prize itself was Mother Teresa's dramatic gesture in persuading the Nobel Committee to forego the customary banquet and save the money for those who really needed the meal. It brought about a flood of emotion. In Norway, of course, but all over Europe people were deeply affected, and the outpouring – which included little children foregoing their pocket money – amounted to almost half the sum of the prize itself. When asked how she proposed to spend the money, she laughed and said, 'I have already spent it in my mind.'

She returned to Calcutta and went into strict retreat for a month, by which time the tumultuous welcome, with bands and fanfares, headlines and receptions, had died down. By the time she emerged, the photographers and journalists had dispersed. But not for long. The country of which she had taken citizenship in 1950 now conferred on her its highest award, the Bharat Ratna. Never before conferred on anyone not born Indian, it had by then been awarded to only 17 of India's most distinguished sons and daughters.

With honours and recognition has come also a degree of criticism and, from some quarters, outright disapproval. Her stand against artificial methods of birth control and abortion, particularly in countries desperately needing to curb population growth, is well known, and there are few takers for her views that she can accommodate all the unwanted children in the

Shishu Bhawans or through adoption services. More serious are the accusations that her mission is to convert people of other faiths to Christianity. I asked her if she did. 'I do convert,' she replied. 'I convert you to a better Hindu, a better Catholic, a better Muslim or Jain or Buddhist. I would like to help you to find God. When you have found Him, it is up to you to do what He wants from you.' On another occasion she wrote, 'You call him Ishwar, some call him Allah, some simply God, but we all have to acknowledge that it is He who made us for greater things: to love and to be loved. Who are we to prevent our people from finding this God who made them – who loves them – to whom they have to return?'

While her own preference is obvious and, like all nuns, she believes herself to be married to Christ, she is no turn-of-the-century evangelist. I am perfectly aware that the babies in Shishu Bhawans are not baptized unless their parentage is known to be Christian, or unless they are to be sent into a Christian house. Since most of the children now go into Hindu homes – the registers carefully maintained are ample proof – it would be unthinkable to baptize such children. Indeed, for her it would be a sin. Similarly, in Kalighat the dying are not administered extreme unction, the last rites performed by a Catholic priest. This is done only to those known to be Catholic or according to a preference expressed.

In late 1995, Mother Teresa was criticized, ironically enough, by several Church leaders in India, for disowning their nationwide campaign to implement a policy whereby a percentage of government jobs be set aside for low-caste Christians. They claimed that Mother Teresa initially gave her blessing, but withdrew it in the face of criticism from the Hindu right-wing. The merits of the issue apart, the attempt by any group to use the respect and

'A board in Kalighat proclaims this to be Mother's first love, which I implicitly believe to be the case.'

NAVIN CHAWLA

undisputed goodwill she enjoys to further a campaign that had a political edge was unnecessary. In the West, meanwhile she was criticized by a few people for being too closely identified with the political right and staunchly opposed to liberation theology; her critics seem to belong to a tradition that see religion as a structure of oppression and regard her in purely political terms. Yet I believe it is not a coincidence that in almost half a century that Mother Teresa has worked around the world, she has never once lent herself to political issues but has, indeed, steered clear of political controversy. I once asked her why, when she could work to further peace, she did not work to lessen war. She said, 'If you are working for peace, that peace lessens war. But I won't mix in politics. War is the fruit of politics, and so I don't involve myself, that's all. If I get stuck in politics, I will stop loving. Because I will have to stand by one, not by all. This is the difference.'

How does one explain this seemingly ordinary woman in everyday terms? She is not a genius or an intellectual. She never attended university or read much beyond the scriptures. She has a good mind and is very hard working and practical, but so are countless millions. Yet the number of people who, because of her, are alive and well today, among them the poor and hungry, sick and destitute, victims of famine and disaster, must run into hundreds of thousands, perhaps millions. There are further millions to whose plight she has lent focus, simply by being there. And there are untold others whom she has in some way inspired. People who have never met her, but have simply read about her, have been motivated to do something themselves. Compared with the vast ocean of charity she has dispensed, the negative side seems minute.

To watch Mother Teresa at prayer is an extraordinary experience, for she is completely at one with her God. She sits on the floor, her legs folded to one

side, her eyes closed. She holds the prayer book in her hands, but she has no need to read from it. She knows each prayer and hymn. As a child in Skopje, she loved to sing and was a member of the church choir. Now her words are merely a whisper. And when, slowly, she bends double to touch her head to the ground in obeisance, her surrender is total.

As a Hindu, armed only with a certain eclecticism, it took me time to understand that Mother Teresa is with Christ in each conscious hour, whether at mass or with each of those she tends. The Christ on her crucifix is no different from the one that lies dying in Kalighat. Neither exists without the other; they are both one. There can be no contradiction in her frequently repeated words that one must reach out to one's neighbour. For Mother Teresa, to love one's neighbour is to love God; if one is unable to love one's neighbour, one is unable to love God. This is what is essential to her, not the size of her mission or the power others may perceive in her. As she once said to me: 'Every Missionary of Charity is the poorest of the poor. But ours is a choice. We completely depend on providence. We don't work for glory or for money. We work for God.'

POPE JOHN PAUL II VISITED NIRMAL HRIDAY,
THE HOME FOR THE DYING, KALIGHAT, IN 1986.
HE WAS DEEPLY MOVED BY THE EXPERIENCE.

PART TWO : THE WORK

*It will be for posterity to decide
whether she is a saint. I can only say that
in a dark time she is a burning and shining light;
in a carnal time, a living embodiment of
Christ's gospel of love; in a godless time,
the Word dwelling among us, full of Grace and truth.*

MALCOLM MUGGERIDGE

SOMETHING BEAUTIFUL FOR GOD,

COLLINS, LONDON, 1971

CHARITY KNOWS NO BOUNDARIES. FOOD, CLOTHING AND
MEDICINES ARE COLLECTED IN INDIA AND OVERSEAS, AND ARE
SENT WHEREVER THERE IS NEED.

A Conversation with Mother Teresa

NAVIN CHAWLA (NC): Mother, as you look over your life, would you say that it has been one of happiness?

MOTHER TERESA (MT): *The happiness that no one can take from me. There has never been a doubt or any unhappiness.*

NC: Are the Sisters from all over India? Are their parents happy?

MT: *The Sisters are from all over India; their parents are very happy to give God their own child, it is a big thing. It has to be a sacrifice also, a very big sacrifice. No, there is no sadness, but a sacrifice. Sacrifice does not cause sadness, especially when you give up to God.*

NC: But sacrifice is a difficult thing.

MT: *No. When you give it to God, there is a greater love. These girls want to give their best. They make to God a total surrender. They give up their position, their house, their parents, their future, dedicating it also to God through the poorest of the poor.*

NC: Over all these years that you have been separated from your own family...

MT: *Where? They have all gone to heaven. There is nobody on earth.*

NC: But over the years, despite the sacrifice, there is the human bond.

MT: *Of course. Naturally, that, nobody can separate. The beautiful thing is that you give it to God and that is very important. 'If you want to give, my disciple, take up the cross,' Jesus says. Very simple, there is no difficulty.*

NC: Does your order expect total obedience?

MT: *Total obedience, wholehearted service, complete poverty and undivided love for Christ. Since the Sisters are going to bind themselves by their vows, they must know what these are going to mean. The vow of obedience means that we have to do God's will in everything. The vow of poverty is very strict in our congregation. We take the vow of chastity, our hearts entirely dedicated to Christ. Finally we take a unique fourth vow — that of giving wholehearted free service to the poor. We cannot work for the rich, nor can we accept any money for our work.*

NC: How is it that all the Sisters look so happy?

MT: *We want the poor to feel loved. We cannot go to them with sad faces. God loves a cheerful giver. He gives most who gives with joy.*

NC: What happens if any of the Sisters feel they have made a mistake in joining?

MT: *They are free to go. But once they have made vows, if they want to go, they can ask permission. Very few have left. It is quite extraordinary that most of our Sisters have been so faithful.*

NC: What about doubts in day-to-day matters, for example, about how work should be structured? Can they come to you?

MT: *We are a normal family, only with big numbers. But we are a normal family, we share everything together, that makes the difference, I think.*

THE NEW CLASSROOM BLOCK AT LORETO CONVENT, ENTALLY.

MOTIJHIL, NOW MUCH IMPROVED, LIES BEHIND IT.

NC: In the midst of great faith can there be doubt, for instance in performing a task?

MT: *It depends for whom you are doing the task. A mother has no doubt when she serves her child. Because she loves. It changes everything in her life. The same thing for us. If we are really in love with Christ, this doubt does not come. Maybe a longing comes to do better, but not doubt. I wouldn't call it a doubt. Doubt disturbs.*

NC: Most of us have doubts. Are we doing the right thing?

MT: *No, that's not a doubt. You want to do greater good for the child. You want to do something better. That's not doubt. Doubt takes away your freedom.*

NC: When one is face to face with someone who is physically maimed, suffering from leprosy, crawling with maggots, then having to touch such a person might cause a doubt.

MT: *That's fear, that's not doubt.*

NC: How is that overcome?

MT: *First of all with prayer, but if you really love that person then it will be easier for you to accept that person and it will be with love and kindness. For that is an opportunity for you to put your love for God in living action. For love begins at home. And for us in our scriptures it is very clearly said. What Jesus said was, 'Whatever you do to the least of my brethren, you do it to me.' If you give a glass of water in my name, you give it to me. I was hungry. I was naked. I was lonely. Faith is a gift of God, which comes*

'If I get stuck in politics, I will stop loving.
Because I will have to stand by one, not by all. '
MOTHER TERESA TO NAVIN CHAWLA

through prayer. The fruit of silence is prayer, the fruit of prayer is faith and the fruit of faith is love, the fruit of love is service and the fruit of service is peace. So it is a whole connection.

NC: From where do you get your strength?

MT: *The mass is the spiritual food that sustains me. I could not pass a single day or hour in my life without it. In the eucharist, I see Christ in the appearance of bread. In the slums, I see Christ in the distressing disguise of the poor — in the broken bodies, in the children, in the dying. That is why this work becomes possible.*

NC: I want to ask you a question which many people who know that I have worked with you in a small way often ask. They say you stand for peace, they also say, whether you like it or not, that you are the world's most powerful woman…

MT: *(interrupts): Do they? I wish I was. Then I will bring peace in the world (laughs).*

NC: You can pick up a telephone and reach a president or a prime minister because you speak in the name of peace.

MT: *In the name of Christ. Without Him I could do nothing.*

NC: Whereas you work to bring about peace, why is it you do not work, they ask, to lessen war?

MT: *If you are working for peace, that peace lessens war. But I won't mix in politics. War is the fruit of politics, and so I don't involve myself, that's all. If I get stuck in politics, I will stop loving. Because I will have to stand by one, not by all. This is the difference.*

NC: Mother, when you go into situations like riots, don't you feel fear?

MT: Fear for what?

NC: Fear for (hesitation)...

MT: Fear for going to God (laughs)!

NC: Or fear for your Sisters?

MT: No, we have given our lives to God (pause). Once we were going to go to Sudan with food, to Southern Sudan. We have our Sisters in Northern Sudan. There was danger of shooting, and the Government did not want us to go. Five of us signed [a declaration] that we were ready to die if the plane was shot down. The next day when we were to leave, [the rebels] said, 'We will shoot the plane.' The pilot refused to go. Otherwise we would have certainly gone.

NC: In the early days, did you have many obstacles? I read about a case when you wanted to start a leprosy colony in Titagarh, local people opposed it because people are afraid of leprosy.

MT: But once they saw, they understood. Even outside India, sometimes we have that opposition, but once they see the work, they understand. You see, when the people come in touch with the poor they realize how beautiful they are.

TO WATCH MOTHER TERESA AT PRAYER IS AN EXTRAORDINARY EXPERIENCE, FOR SHE IS COMPLETELY AT ONE WITH HER GOD.

'In the Eucharist, I see Christ in the appearance of bread. In the slums,
I see Christ in the distressing disguise of the poor… That is why this work becomes possible.'

MOTHER TERESA TO NAVIN CHAWLA

NC: Aren't you spreading yourself too thin, channelling your missions and opening houses in so many countries?

MT: *Because we are Missionaries of Charity, and a missionary is a person who has to go and spread the good news, it makes no difference. Today in India, tomorrow in Europe, anywhere the voice of God calls you. And a missionary is a person who is sent to become a carrier of God's love. That's why we are Missionaries of Charity. Double. Like somebody said to me, 'You are spoiling the poor by giving everything to them.' Then I said, 'Nobody has spoiled us more than God Himself.' Because He is also giving. And another person said to me, 'Why do you give them the fish to eat? Why don't you give them a rod to catch the fish?' So I replied, 'My people, when I pick them up, they can't even stand. They are either sick or hungry. So I take them. Once they are all right, they don't come to me any more, for they can stand on their own!'*

NC: What about the suffering co-workers?

MT: *Yes, the suffering co-workers are sick persons who adopt one of our Sisters. If you are sick, and you have got me and you offer all your pain and all your suffering for me, you offer that to God for me, for the work I do. And I offer the work, and my love of God for you. I help you and you help me. And we become second selves to each other. It is a tremendous gift. You cannot go out to work, so I do the working and you do the suffering. I have a person who does that for me, she has had so many operations already. She offers every operation for me, while I go running about the place for her. She is in terrible pain but she offers everything for me. We have an understanding that we share everything together. That is the bond. She, with suffering, I, with work and prayers. Beautiful. Every Sister has a sick person praying for her.*

NC: So you get extra strength, and you give that to your work.

MT: *Yes, yes, and they get extra strength from our prayers, from our work, from the sacrifices we make. Beautiful.*

NC: And the other co-workers?

MT: *We have family of almost 400,000 co-workers in the world, who come and share the work with the Sisters. I give them the opportunity to touch the poor and the lonely. Loneliness is worse in many ways than physical poverty. Many people of all faiths come to me, not merely to give a donation, but to do work with their hands. Then we have doctors, medical co-workers who come to the dispensaries and they take care of the sick; youth co-workers who spread the love for the poor among the youth, love for purity, love for prayer, they share that among the youth. Youth, they are looking for a challenge. Sometimes they are misled. Lots of them are really longing for God. Look at all the volunteers from all over the world. They come to serve here for two or three months. They work during the whole year to earn money, because we give them nothing, so they have to pay for everything.*

NC: An interesting thing I have always observed in Kalighat is that there are many people there, maybe a hundred, some close to death, but no one seems afraid of death.

MT: *You feel the presence of God there, and they feel the love they get. Like one of them said, 'I've lived like an animal in the street but I will die like an angel', with love and care. They die content; 23,000 have died there.*

NC: What is their greatest enemy, is it rejection?

MT: *Poverty. They don't have anything. They have no one. They have nothing. They are street cases. We don't take anyone else, only the sick and dying destitutes; they have to be from the street. We don't take house cases. In Prem Dan maybe some of our slum cases are there, but in Kalighat we don't take anybody else. Prem Dan, have you been there? You should go there.*

NC: You once said to me that the greatest fear a human being can face is the fear of humiliation.

MT: *The surest way to be one with God is to accept humiliation.*

NC: Have you encountered humiliation?

MT: *Oh, yes, plenty. This publicity is also humiliation.*

NC: Is it humiliation, or is it the acceptance of your work for the poor?

MT: *Humiliation, because we know we have nothing ourselves. You see what God has done. I think God is wanting to show His greatness by using nothingness.*

NC: So all these awards that you have received, the Nobel Prize for instance?

MT: *I don't even remember the number. They are nothing. Of the Nobel Prize, I said I will accept it if you give it for the glory of God and in the name of the poor. I do not accept awards in my name. I am nothing.*

NC: You did not allow the traditional banquet to take place after the Nobel investiture?

MT: *No. Instead they gave me the money for it. So we had a big dinner for 2,000 poor people on Christmas Day with that money. That was much better. In Delhi, they gave me a reception and they prepared dinner. I made them all go to Nirmal Hriday, and they fed the people. All the ministers and the big people went there and fed our people.*

NC: Do the leprosy patients continue to be the most rejected people?

MT: *Not now. Because we have medicine. And if they come in time we can cure them. But being unwanted is the most terrible disease that human beings can experience. The only cure can lie in willing hands to serve and hearts to go on loving them.*

NC: And are they able to go back into society?

MT: *Yes, yes. If they come in time. Everywhere we have land to rehabilitate them. In India, we have quite a number of homes: in Delhi, Lucknow, Ranchi, Asansol, Calcutta, many places. The Government has given big amounts of land, we buy the material and give it to the leprosy family. They often build their own houses. In many countries people give us land or a house. Like in Nicaragua, someone gave us a house; in Budapest, someone gave us a house.*

NC: You have been working in Calcutta for so many years. Has this work changed people's perceptions?

MT: *It has brought many people to love each other better, and that's more important.*

NC: Are there fewer destitute people now than when you started?

MT: *I don't know (laughs). I could not tell you that. But those who die with us, die in peace. For me that is the greatest development of the human life, to die in peace and in dignity, for that's for eternity.*

NC: I want to ask you a difficult question. You have built up a very large network, and that network is associated with you.

MT: *(interrupts): How? It is associated with the whole society, the whole congregation.*

NC: Yes, but since you are its foundress, you are synonymous with the Missionaries of Charity.

MT: *That is all right. But only together, with the Sisters.*

NC: With you as organizational head.

MT: *That's right. It has to be like that. In your family you are the one. That is the same with us. That is the recognition that has to be given, otherwise there would be confusion.*

NC: But Mother, after you have gone…

MT: *Let me go first (we laugh). Just as God has found me, He will find somebody else. The work is God's work, and He will see to it.*

NC: Mother, why are you going up and down the stairs so much [she has a heart problem]? I am sure this is against the doctor's advice.

MT: *(with a laugh): There is no time to think of it.*

NC: I saw a picture of you in a magazine. You were being shown around the White House in Washington, and you looked as if you were overwhelmed.

MT: *I was thinking there was so much room. I feel like taking all my poor people, and filling houses. Seeing the emptiness, I always feel like wanting to fill it (laughs).*

NC: With all this difficult work, how do you still manage a sense of humour?

MT: *But the work is very, very beautiful, you know. We have no reason to be unhappy. We are doing it with Jesus, for Jesus, to Jesus. We are really contemplatives in the heart of the world. Jesus said, whatever you do to the least of my brethren, you do to me. If you give a glass of water in my name, you give it to me. If you receive a little child in my name, you receive me. That is why I want to receive all these unborn children. God's own image is in every single child, no matter what that child is, disabled or beautiful or ugly — it's God's beautiful image created for greater things — to love and be loved. That is why you and I and all of us must insist to preserve the gift of God, for it is something very beautiful. That little one who is unwanted and unloved, who has come into the world already unwanted, what a terrible suffering that is! Today it is the greatest disease, to be unwanted, unloved, just left alone, a throwaway of society.*

NC: Mother, you told me a beautiful story once, about a woman of Calcutta who shared her rice.

MT: *Yes, I remember. I was not surprised that she gave. This is natural. Poor people are always sharing. But I was surprised that she knew that her neighbours were hungry. People often hide, especially people who have seen better days. Like, a man came here one day. He had been better off before. He had come down in life. He came here one day. He said, 'Mother Teresa, I cannot eat that food that is being given there.' Then I said to him, 'I am eating it every day.' And he looked at me and said, 'You are eating it?' and I said, 'Yes.' Then he said, 'I will eat also.' My eating it gave him courage to accept the humiliation. If I could not have said that, maybe he would have remained hard and bitter inside, and not accepted anything. But when he knew that I was with him he was encouraged…*

NC: Is poverty your strength?

MT: *We do not accept anything, neither church maintenance, nor salary, nor anything for the work we do, all over the world. Every Missionary of Charity is the poorest of the poor. That is why we can do anything. Whatever is given to the poor is the same for us. We wear the kind of clothes they wear. But ours is a choice. We choose that way. To be able to understand the poor, we must know what is poverty. Otherwise we will speak another language, no? We won't be able to come close to that mother who is anxious for her child. We completely depend on providence. We are like the trees, like the flowers. But we are more important to Him than the flowers or the grass. He takes care of them, He takes much greater care of us. That is the beautiful part of the congregation.*

NC: What makes you sad?

MT: *When I see people suffer, it makes me sad. The physical suffering of it.*

NC: How do you view your achievements?

MT: *There is no answer to that. We must not spoil God's work. We don't work for glory or for money. The Sisters are consecrated people. It's a consecrated love. It is all for Jesus. We work for God. Accha, I must run now.*

NAVIN CHAWLA
Mother Teresa, *Sinclair-Stevenson, London, 1992*

OPPOSITE:
'*Total obeisance, whole-hearted service, complete poverty and undivided love for Christ. Since the Sisters are going to bind themselves by their vows, they must know what these are going to mean.*'
MOTHER TERESA TO NAVIN CHAWLA

Their life is tough and austere by worldly standards, certainly; yet I never met such delightful, happy women, or such an atmosphere of joy as they create. Mother Teresa, as she is fond of explaining, attaches the utmost importance to this joyousness. The poor, she says, deserve not just service and dedication, but also the joy that belongs to human love. This is what the Sisters give them abundantly. Today, notoriously, the religious orders are short of vocations. Nor is the shortage being rectified by permitting nuns to use lipstick, wear mini-habits, and otherwise participate in the ways and amenities of contemporary affluence. The Missionaries of Charity, on the other hand, are multiplying at a fantastic rate. Their Calcutta house is bursting at the seams, and as each new house is opened there are volunteers clamouring to go there. As the whole story of Christendom shows, if everything is asked for, everything — and more — will be accorded; if little, then nothing. It is curious, when this is so obvious, that nowadays the contrary proposition should seem the more acceptable, and endeavour be directed towards softening the austerities of the service of Christ and reducing its hazards with a view to attracting people into it. After all, it was in kissing a leper's hideous sores that St Francis found the gaiety to captivate the world and gather round him some of the most audacious spirits of the age, to whom he offered only the glory of being naked on the naked earth for Christ's sake. If the demands had been less, so would the response have been. I should never have believed it possible, knowing India as I do over a number of years, to induce Indian girls of good family to tend outcasts and untouchables brought in from Calcutta streets, yet this, precisely, is the very first task that Mother Teresa gives them to do when they come to her as postulants. They do it, not just in obedience, but cheerfully and ardently, and gather round her in ever greater numbers for the privilege of doing it.

MALCOLM MUGGERIDGE
Something Beautiful for God, *Collins, London, 1971*

SISTERS AND
NOVICES AT A SPECIAL
CEREMONY IN
CALCUTTA WHERE
SOME SISTERS MADE
THEIR FINAL VOWS.

Make us worthy Lord to serve
our fellow men through the
world who live and die in
poverty and hunger. Give them
through our hands, this day
their daily bread and by
our understanding love
give peace and joy

'Sacrifice, to be real
Must cost
Must hurt
Must empty
us of ourselves.'
MOTHER TERESA

MOTHER TERESA
PURPOSEFULLY CLIMBS
DOWN THE STAIRS AT
MOTHERHOUSE.

'I thirst.'

Inscribed on every crucifix in every house of the Missionaries of Charity are the words 'I thirst'. They recall both Jesus' words on the cross and, more symbolically, his cry of spiritual love and acceptance. If two words had to be chosen to sum up the life and work of the Missionaries of Charity then it would be these. They serve as a constant reminder to each member of the society that their lives are woven about the Eucharist. Each morning at mass when bread is broken, it is the body of Christ that is wounded, and each time the wine is poured, it is His blood that is being shared. The Sisters live the mass in those they tend, for it is here that they quench the 'infinite thirst of Jesus' by a life of prayer, contemplation and penance, by serving Christ in His distressing disguise.

'In the mass we have Jesus in the appearance of bread, while in the slums we touch Him in the broken bodies and in the abandoned children,' Mother Teresa often says. In so doing, the Missionaries of Charity are prepared to accept humiliation, suffering and even death.

Mother Teresa's response to her call meant that it was no longer wholly sufficient to observe the three vows of chastity, poverty and obedience that the Loreto Order imposed on their congregation. Instead she waited impatiently for two years to be permitted to take an even stricter fourth vow of 'wholehearted and free service to the poorest of the poor'. This vow would bind the Missionaries of Charity, without counting the cost of the hard labour involved, joyfully and without expectation, actually and spiritually to feed, clothe, shelter and nurse those who had lost all faith and hope in life. The call and the inspiration sheets made it abundantly clear that they must reach out to the destitute on the streets, which was obviously not possible from behind convent walls. Invariably, the Sisters refer to this fourth vow as 'our way'.

On 7 October 1950, the constitutions were approved by the sacred congregation in Rome. Father van Exem read the Decree of Erection during a mass celebrated by Archbishop Perier himself. It began thus: 'For more than two years now, a small group of young women under the guidance of Sister Teresa, a lawfully uncloistered religious of the Institute of the Blessed Virgin Mary, have devoted themselves…to helping the poor, the children, the adults, the aged and the sick, in this, our Metropolitan City.'

The decree went on to spell out the fourth vow in greater detail. It spoke of the additional requirement 'to devote themselves out of abnegation to the care of the poor and needy who, crushed by want and destitution, live in conditions unworthy of human dignity. Those who join this institute, therefore, are resolved to spend themselves unremittingly in seeking out, in towns and villages, even amid squalid surroundings, the poor, the abandoned, the sick, the infirm, the dying…'

Mother was to tell me on many occasions, 'If we did not believe that this was the body of Christ, we would never be able to do this work. No amount of money could make us do it. It is He whom we reach in the people who are unwanted, unemployed, uncared for; they seem useless to society, nobody has time for them. It is you and I who must find them and help them. Often we pass them without seeing them. But they are there for the finding.'

MISSIONARIES OF CHARITY
54A ACHARYA J. CHANDRA BOSE
CALCUTTA 700016, INDIA

J.D.M.

My dearest children, Sisters Brothers, Fathers, Lay Missionaries Co-workers.

This brings you my prayer and blessing for each one of you - my love and gratitude to each one of you for all you have been and have done all these 40 years. to share the joy of loving each other and the Poorest of the Poor.

Your presence and the work you have done throughout the world for the glory of God and the good of the Poor has been a living miracle of love of God and yours in action. God has shown His greatness by

using nothingness - so let us always remain in our nothingness - so as to give God free hand to use us without consulting us.

Let us accept whatever He gives and give whatever He takes with a big smile

As the days of the General Chapter draw near my heart is filled with joy and expectation - of the beautiful things God will do through each one of you by accepting with joy the One God has chosen to be our Superior General Beautiful are the ways of G. If we allow Him to use us as He wants.

- over -

'In her eyes, the person who, in the accepted sense, is the recipient, is also the giver and the one who gives the most.'

CHAIRMAN OF THE NORWEGIAN NOBEL COMMITTEE, 1979

109

2.

MISSIONARIES OF CHARITY
54A ACHARYA J. CHANDRA BOSE
CALCUTTA 700016, INDIA.

I am still in Eastern Europe. The living Miracles God has "during these days have been a proof of His tender for His MC. and our Poor.

Let our gratitude be our strong resolution to be only all for Jesus through Mary. Let us be Pure and Humble like Mary and we are sure to be Holy like Jesus.

Humility always is the root of zeal for souls and charity. We see that in Jesus - on the Cross and in the Eucharist. We see it in Mary - went in haste to serve as hand Maid - not as Mother of God.

so it is very important for us MC. to be pure and humble. No MC. can live a true MC. life and the 4th vow without a pure and humble heart. because a pure heart can see God in the Poor - a humble heart can love and serve Jesus in the Poor.

Remember the five fingers
You - did - it - to - Me

Remember - Love begins at home - our Community - our family.

Remember - Works of love are works of Peace.

Let us thank Jesus for the 40 years of tender love we have received from Him through each other - and pray that we

3.   MISSIONARIES OF CHARITY
                     54A ACHARYA J·CHANDRA BOSE
                       CALCUTTA 700016, INDIA

grow in this love for each other and our Poor – by deepening our personal and intimate love for Jesus and greater attachment to Jesus through Prayer and Sacrifice.

Try to be Jesus' love, Jesus compassion – Jesus presence to each other and the Poor you serve.

All this will be possible if you keep close to Mary the Mother of Jesus and our Mother. She will guide & protect you and keep you only all for Jesus.

Let nothing and nobody ever separate you from the love of Jesus and Mary – It was at Her pleading that the Society was born – let it be again at Her pleading that the Society gives Saints to Mother Church.

Remember wherever you may be – Mother's prayer love and Blessing will always be with you

God bless you
                        Mc Teresa mc

MOTHER TERESA AT HER DESK IN KALIGHAT.

111

K alu, for that is his nickname, is about 70 years old. He has only stumps for limbs. At first glance he is head and torso alone, propped up in a child's handcart against a supporting wall. From a distance he looks like an infant with a wizened head. Despite life's unending adversities, Kalu is usually cheerful. But not today, I can see that from afar. Kalu was once a respected member of a reasonably well-to-do farming family in South India. He was one of four brothers. He was still a young man when he noticed a patch on his back. He showed it to a doctor in a nearby town, who diagnosed leprosy. Filled with horror, he rushed instinctively to the temple to beseech Lord Vishnu to spare him. What sin, Lord, had he committed in which previous incarnation, that so severe a punishment was being meted on him? He lay prostrate before the Lord as his body was wracked with sobs.

God, he believed, soon revealed himself in the form of a soothsayer, who sold him a 'special' medicine that would cure him in a matter of weeks. From soothsayer to astrologer, to an old woman who sold him magic potions, he went secretly to distant towns in search of a cure. He did not reveal his secret to his brothers. For two years, he hid the terrible truth until one day, inevitably, a tell-tale patch appeared on his right hand. The discovery was met with horror. It was clear to his family that this

THE MISSIONARIES OF CHARITY MUST TAKE A SPECIAL, FOURTH VOW TO SERVE THE POOREST OF THE POOR.

112

was a divine visitation for sins committed. They remembered all too well the last case of leprosy in their village, a few years earlier, which had caused the village elders to banish the offending family. If the truth about Kalu were to be known, they would lose their status in the village. Who would marry their daughters? The brothers took a decision to isolate Kalu in a small shed at the bottom of the fields. When Kalu refused to comply – for he was part owner of the 20 acres of land the brothers jointly farmed – he was trussed up like a chicken and taken there in the dead of night. His brothers chained him to the floor, and threw some food for him into a metal bowl.

Unable to bear the humiliation, one night he broke the chain and ran away, never to return. For months he wandered like a sick animal, sometimes to this town, sometimes to that, begging for food at bus stops, railway stations and outside temples. Medical treatment was irregular and infrequent. In a matter of a few years, nerve damage overtook his once beautifully shaped fingers until, one horror-filled afternoon, his by now benumbed and ulcerated hands were amputated in some anonymous jail hospital, it no longer mattered where. Sick at heart, more dead than alive, he found his way to Delhi. There he learned of Mother Teresa's home for leprosy patients. That was five years ago. Now he is among friends, and is usually cheerful. After years of living like an animal, Kalu has once again found a little dignity and some peace.

NAVIN CHAWLA
Mother Teresa, *Sinclair-Stevenson, London, 1992*

'A medical mission'

Sister Andrea runs the outpatient department at Shishu Bhawan. At 21, she decided to join the Missionaries of Charity. Her father, a professional man in Freiburg in Germany was 'shattered'; he had high hopes for his daughter and he wanted her to become a doctor or a lawyer. Her mother said, 'You can't do this to us'. But her mind was made up. When Sister Andrea arrived in India, Mother Teresa decided that she should train for medicine. She was horrified: she could not stand the sight of blood. The first time she was exposed to surgery, she fainted in the operating theatre. But Mother was insistent and so, five years later, she joined the ranks of Sister Gertrude and Sister Shanti and became a qualified medical practitioner. Now most mornings find her in her clinic, with as many as 4,000 patients huddled in groups outside waiting to see her or her team of 30 Sisters. Many well-known Calcutta specialists also volunteer their services. They are not merely generous, they are also 'punctual to the minute', high praise indeed from an efficient German nun.

Today is Wednesday, so it is the general dispensary day. There must be at least 600 patients, divided into groups for dispensing, dressings, injections and general examinations. There is no noise and everyone, including the patients, seems to know where to stand or sit, and what to do. I enter Sister Andrea's small examination room. A young man has brought in his grandfather. Sister recommends an X-ray and a sputum test. Who will pay for it, I ask? 'We will,' she replies, 'but many hospitals and clinics are very good to us and charge only fifty per cent of their normal rates.' Munni Begum, aged 30, is next. She is asked to attend the gynaecology clinic on Friday. All

THE MISSIONARIES OF CHARITY RUN SEVERAL MOBILE MEDICAL CAMPS IN AND AROUND CALCUTTA, AND IN SEVERAL OTHER CITIES BESIDES.

the while, buses and trams clatter noisily on the road outside. 'Our daily music,' says Sister Andrea with a smile.

This is just one of 20 dispensaries, some of them mobile, which the Missionaries of Charity run in Calcutta and the surrounding villages. It was until recently a jumble of old buildings until a Hindu benefactor gave Mother Teresa the money to pull down the dilapidated structures and put up a cluster of brand new buildings. 'Earlier, we never had enough space inside and I always felt so bad that our patients had to queue up outside, sometimes in the hot sun, sometimes in pouring rain. Now everyone can be accommodated inside. I cannot tell you how much I prayed for this.'

A loud racking cough announced the next patient. Nepal Haldar was a young man of 22, clearly suffering from tuberculosis. Thirty-five per cent of all her patients had TB, said Sister Andrea. The drugs needed were expensive. It cost about 300 rupees to provide Nepal Haldar with one month's supply of rifampicin, vitamins, tonics and food. There were conditions attached. He would have to attend the clinic every month, and bring back the empty shells, as evidence that he had actually consumed the medicine.

The following day I accompanied Sisters Gertrude and Andrea and their team of 30 Sisters and novices to the village of Kheora Pukur, 20 miles from Calcutta. From early morning, neatly labelled wooden boxes were filled with different medicines, which were then loaded into a large truck, which proclaimed in neat blue letters 'Missionaries of Charity (Mother Teresa)' on both sides. Into the truck were also placed several wooden benches, which accommodated the Sisters for their journey. When we reached our destination – a church compound in the village – at least 2,000 people were awaiting the team's arrival. Within minutes, the Sisters set themselves up in the four available rooms; the patients knew which queues to join. One room became a simple operation theatre. Malnutrition was the main culprit; but here were plenty of cases of skin disorders, respiratory diseases and digestive problems. In the midst of all the medicines being dispensed, I was amused to find large cartons of chocolates. I learned that a European labour minister had visited India with a view to recommending a ban on exports related to child labour. During the course of his visit to India he called on Mother Teresa, who showed him some of the realities of life in the streets. The Sisters had no idea

what he recommended, but he did send Mother Teresa seven tons of chocolates, and 12,000 delighted children had already enjoyed eating them at her different centres.

I could not stay as long as I wished. An old man had hobbled in with a bandage tied to his right foot. Sister Gertrude bent down to open it. Inside I saw a large gaping wound, crawling with maggots. Painstakingly and in spite of the stench, she pulled them out one by one with tweezers. Then she disinfected the wound and tied a clean bandage. She asked me to take him to Kalighat, because he needed further treatment and rest, for his body was racked with fever. All the while we drove back in my car to Kalighat he did not utter a sound. It was only as the driver and I were helping him inside that he whispered three words: 'Angels from Heaven,' he said.

'It is difficult for the poor to reach us: we must go to them.'
MOTHER TERESA TO NAVIN CHAWLA

*The feeding programme, Shishu Bhawan, Calcutta. This
is one of several such centres run by the Missionaries
of Charity around the world.*

BY SEVEN EACH MORNING, a queue begins to form outside the blue-painted metal doors of Shishu Bhawan at 78 Acharya JC Bose Road in Calcutta. This morning there must be about 800 people, many of them women with children clustering around them. This is one of seven centres in Calcutta where the Missionaries of Charity give the poor a nourishing meal. Each recipient carries a card that identifies him or her and names the feeding centre.

Inside, the large courtyard has been cleared of the ambulances and vans that I saw parked yesterday. Instead everywhere there are large vats of *khitchri* (kedgeree), rice mixed with lentils and vegetables, that are ladled out by the Sisters. The actual preparation of the food begins at midnight; food here is cooked for about a thousand. On days when the number exceeds the food supply, the Sisters offer bread or some rice. No one is allowed to go away empty-handed. I learn that almost the same number of poor are fed in the other centres. In the afternoon, another long queue begins to form. These people, too, are needy, but they are not homeless. They have some means to cook and so are given dry rations – rice, wheat and some oil.

While the Sisters went about their work methodically, I spoke to Nasir Ahmed, who had just finished his meal. When I asked him to sit with me on the bench, he shook his head. He said that he got more pleasure from sitting on the ground. Aged 72, he could no longer see well, and now found it difficult to get employment. He had been attending this centre for about three years. Sometimes he helped the Sisters with their work, doing a little fetching and carrying. His wife had died. He had no children. As we talked, he gestured to me to bend down to listen to him. In a whisper he confided that the food seldom varied, and he found it somewhat tasteless. I nodded understandingly. After a few moments of reflection he said, almost to himself, 'If the Sisters and volunteers can eat it, well, so can I. And it keeps away the pangs of hunger.' His friend Haripodo Mandal, who was once a rickshaw puller, heard that remark and nodded. He said, 'I married very late, and I have four small children. Sometimes when I am not able to collect my rations, I have to beg for a few rupees. If I don't get anything, my children would starve that night. But I know that if I knock on these doors even in the middle of the night, no Sister will send me away without a little something. Sometimes it is only a packet of biscuits or milk for the children, but that night we don't go hungry.'

'Two Buddhist monks from Japan came to see me some years ago. I told them that we have a practice that on Fridays none of us eats during the day, and with the money that is saved, we buy food for the poor. I did not know that when they went back to Japan, they told other monks about it. Soon the word spread and many people began to give up a meal a day and put the money aside. One day they sent me all the money they had collected. Wonderful, no? With that I was able to build another floor of the building for the [mentally disturbed] girls in Tengra [in Calcutta] which you saw yesterday. Then I was able to take a hundred more women from the jail. In fact twenty-two more are coming next week. God has such wonderful ways of providing.'

'I have never been in need but I accept whatever people give me for the poor. I never refuse them because they have a right to give in charity. I accept whatever. I only feel angry when I see people throwing away things that we could use.'

'What we are doing is nothing but a drop in the ocean. But if we didn't do it, the ocean would be less because of that missing drop. I do not agree with the big way of doing things. To me what matters is an individual. To get to love the person we must come in close contact with him or her. If we wait till we get the numbers, then we will be lost in numbers. And we will never be able to show the love and respect for that person. Every person is Christ for me, and since there is only one Jesus, that person is the one person in the world at that moment.'

'There are many types of hunger. Sometimes I find it easier to give a plate of rice and satisfy that hunger. But there is a much deeper hunger. That is for love. There is terrible loneliness in being unwanted, abandoned by everybody. You find such people sleeping in the streets of London, New York, Madrid and other cities. Sometimes they are 'shut-ins', people who are in their houses but still unwanted and unloved; living lives of such loneliness, known not by their names but the numbers of their rooms.'

MOTHER TERESA
in conversation with Navin Chawla
Calcutta, 24 March 1996

'What we are doing is nothing but a drop in the ocean. But if we didn't do it, the ocean would be less because of that missing drop.'
MOTHER TERESA

I look back on the days I spent with Mother Teresa in Calcutta as golden ones. Talking with her was a constant delight. She lets things out casually; as that she bought a printing-press for the lepers so that they could print pamphlets and leaflets and make a little money. How, in God's name, I asked myself, did she know what press to buy and where to buy it? And with those stumps, how could the lepers hope to set type? Fatuous questions! The press is there and working; the lepers are delighted with it. She has, I found, a geography of her own — a geography of compassion. Somehow she hears that in Venezuela there are abandoned poor; so off the Sisters go there, and a house is set up. Then that in Rome — in this case, from the Pope himself — there are derelicts, as in Calcutta. Or again, that in Australia the aboriginals and half-castes need love and care. In each case, wherever it may be, the call is heard and answered.

When she is away in Europe or America, she only longs to be back in Calcutta with her poor. These are her beloved. Walking with her among them, queuing at the dispensary, crowding round her at the leper settlement, I kept hearing the muttered word 'Mother!' It wasn't that they had anything to say to her or to ask her; just that they wanted to establish contact with her, to know she was there. I quite understood. The Sisters likewise need her presence and, when they are stationed away from Calcutta, long for her visits. Visiting the other houses in India, the first question always was: 'When will she come?'

To me, Mother Teresa represents, essentially, love in action, which is surely what Christianity is about. Perhaps, I say to myself, the geneticists and family-planners will succeed in constructing a broiler-house set-up where a Mother Teresa would be unneeded and unheeded. Even then, though, there will be some drop-outs with wounds that need healing, wants that need satisfying, souls that need saving. There she and the Sisters will be; just as, however thickly and substantially the concrete is laid down, somewhere, somehow, there is a crack through which a tiny green shoot breaks out to remind us that this life of which we are a part is indestructible, and has its origins and its fulfilment elsewhere.

MALCOLM MUGGERIDGE
Something Beautiful for God, *Collins, London, 1971*

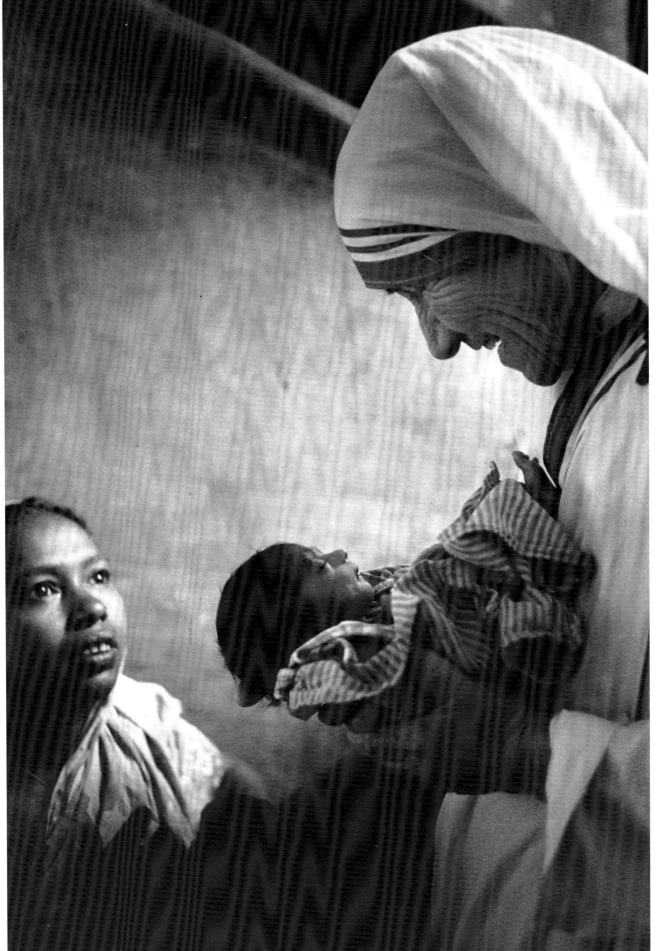

'A child is their only joy in life. The rich have so many other things. If you remove a child from the home of the poor, or those with leprosy, who is going to smile at them? Who is going to help them get better?'

MOTHER TERESA
ON LEPROSY PATIENTS
WHO SOMETIMES INFECT
THEIR CHILDREN

28th
48
Motijhil - At 9 a.m there were about 21 children waiting   We started school out in the open. Monica took the big children and I took the younger ones. The little ones were dirty and untidy. - but very happy.- After about an hour or so.- we went round to see more families. I found many. I treated the sick - which were not so many and on my way to St Teresa's I went to see

a TB patient who had asked for me.- Very poor and with very high fever.- After tiffin & prayers. with Anne & Satiti we went to Miss Roy the Inspectress of Schools She was ready to give a grant for the school I told her that I wanted to teach the children the things they need most- and that so I wanted to be free. She agreed with everything I said & told me to see Mr Mozumder for whom she gave me a very nice letter He was extremely nice- but unable to help, from his own quarters. As the work is so very necessary- he adviced to meet the Minister of Education & Relief. and insist with them for immediate help

29th
48
Motijhil - The children were already waiting for me at the foot of the bridge there were 41 - much cleaner. those who were not clean I gave them a good wash at the tank - We had Catechism after the 1st lesson on hygiene - then reading- I laughed a good many times - As I had never taught little children before.

'The miracle is that every day many families, and in India mainly Hindu families, come and adopt our children. Thousands and thousands have gone to such loving homes.'

MOTHER TERESA

'I have never refused a child. Never. Not one.'

MOTHER TERESA
TO NAVIN CHAWLA

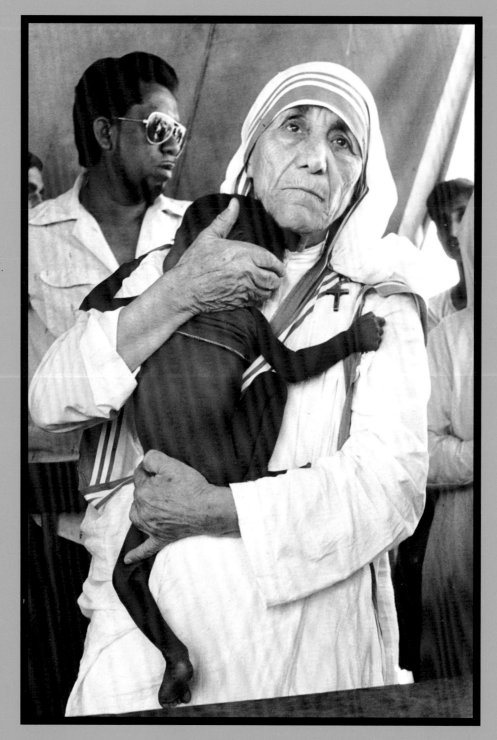

the - To at did not go so well. We used the ground instead of a black board – Everybody was delighted – after the needle work class – we went to visit the sick – We were called in to a Muslim para - to see a child and old woman – and also a Hindu family – the Mother is dying of T.B. They asked me to go often and see her. I came home early to be able to do more writing I shall stay in for my day of recollection.

29th
(30th) We had class. books. slates were used – the children were delighted. We went to see New Review Office not given. Went to Tiljola everyone came for the instruction out in the open.

Jan. 1949
1st New - year – We had no school – I went to see Mrs. Das Gupta – Social worker – after noon wrote & went to the I.H.M. meeting

2nd Children from Motijhil came to 9 am. mass 20 Exposition – wrote rules.

3rd Motijhil – Sabina an old girl from St. Mary's a trained teacher insisted on helping – so

she came with me – she took the children Monica took hers and Lucy took the little ones To Nicaise paid us a visit – he was pleased at the "real thing" 10 New children Muslim came I went round to see the sick – I found Mrs. Jensen Protestant old lady. – She does not want God because he does not hear her prayers. she has given up praying. – What misery – her son is mad I shall try to make come with me to the home before I left she said a few little prayers just to please me. Poor old lady.

I discovered the impact of Mother Teresa quite early in our acquaintance. I had not seen her for several months, as she had been on an extended visit abroad, then one day I received news that she was to arrive from Rome that very evening. It was not certain how long she would stay in Delhi, so I decided to go to the airport to meet her. The Air India flight from Rome landed 15 minutes late, and by the time Mother Teresa reached the terminal building it was almost 7.30pm.

'I am glad you have come,' she said, greeting me with a smile. 'You must make sure I catch the plane to Calcutta tonight.'

I did not think that this was possible, and pointed out that the flight to Calcutta departed from the domestic terminal. The scheduled departure was 8pm; aggravatingly, the flight was on time and Mother Teresa's luggage was not yet off the Air India plane. I was still new to this phenomenon called Mother Teresa, and had not reckoned with her determination. In any case, what she went on to say was sobering enough.

'There is a child dying in Shishu Bhawan in Calcutta. I am carrying in my luggage an experimental drug that might save the child's life. You must help me to catch the flight,' she said softly. She had pulled her rosary from the old cloth bag she carried, and began to pray. Watching her made me considerably nervous. It was now past 7.45pm, and the flight to Calcutta had boarded.

Meanwhile, several people in the terminal building, aware of Mother Teresa's presence, were coming up to her to be blessed, for autographs, and just to be near her. But word had spread that a child lay dying in Calcutta and needed Mother Teresa desperately. I learned later that the airport staff, from senior managers to humble porters, had sped in every direction to help. Suddenly, Mother Teresa's luggage, which consisted of six cardboard boxes (one of which contained her personal effects and the rest medicines), rumbled in on the conveyor belt, the very first pieces of luggage to be brought in. As if from nowhere, someone placed a boarding card in her hand. Unknown to us, the control tower had had a word with the captain of the

flight, who was just then taxiing towards the runway. The captain, a Calcutta man himself, brought the aircraft to a halt. Flight control warned air traffic of a slight change. The aircraft was now ready for Mother Teresa. Would I be so kind as to drive her to the aircraft in my car? A few minutes later, a ladder emerged through the mist, the aircraft door opened and Mother Teresa, with her boxes of medicines, boarded the flight to Calcutta.

Ten days later, Mother Teresa was in Delhi again. My first question, of course, was about the child in Shishu Bhawan. Her face wreathed in smiles, Mother Teresa told me that she had reached Calcutta just in time. The child was well on its way to recovery. 'It was a first-class miracle, wasn't it?' she said.

'It was a first-class miracle wasn't it?'
MOTHER TERESA

NAVIN CHAWLA
Mother Teresa, *Sinclair-Stevenson,*
London, 1992

A PROSPECTIVE PARENT WITH A CHILD AT

THE ADOPTION CENTRE, SHISHU BHAWAN, DELHI.

'This work is my life'

The Nirmala Shishu Bhawan is really two large buildings located at 77 and 78 Acharya JC Bose Road in Calcutta. For widely different reasons, they are well known to the city police and the municipality, to almost all clinics and hospitals, and to people from all walks of life, from the affluent to the poor and hungry. For this is a multi-purpose centre where several different activities are carried out.

The day begins with the feeding programme, when a thousand destitute people queue up outside the blue-painted gates to receive a cooked meal. While the final stragglers are being fed, Sister Andrea, the German doctor, and her team of medical Sisters set up their outpatient department which lasts into the early afternoon. Hardly does that end before the distribution of dry rations begins. While this is going on, the adoption clinic, run by a special group of Sisters and operating four times a week, sees a constant flow of social workers and prospective parents, mainly middle-class Hindu families.

Meanwhile in number 77 and the first floor of number 78, almost 400 children, ranging from infants barely one month old to children up to six or seven, are cared for by Sisters, volunteers and some paid workers. Some of these tiny creatures, abandoned on doorsteps or in the streets, have been brought here by the police or passers-by. Others have been delivered without explanation by clinics. Many are found by the Sisters as they scour the streets. A few are even discovered left bundled up outside the blue gates of Shishu Bhawan.

As Sister José took me onto the verandah of number 77, I found myself in a nursery where about 30 toddlers were being looked after by some Sisters assisted by several volunteers. Within a few seconds, half a dozen children attached themselves to my knees, while many more clutched onto Sister José's sari, clamouring for her attention with cries of 'titter, titter', meaning, of course, 'Sister'. Further movement was rendered almost impossible, and it took several minutes to reach the adjacent room, where the two- and three-year-olds had their play space. No sooner had that door been opened than confusion ensued, as these children, too, rushed at Sister José. As the Sisters and volunteers tried to calm them down, I noticed that the children looked remarkably healthy. Many were dressed identically: someone had donated whole bundles of curtain material, which the deft tailors in Shishu Bhawan had soon transformed into neat little dresses and shorts to fit the required sizes.

To prevent the children climbing up to the first floor, a large bench blocked the way to the stairs. Sister José suggested that we climb over it, a wise precaution, because I could see the adventurous glint in several pairs of eyes.

The scene upstairs was quite different. Here lay 172 infants in their cribs. It was feed time, so most of them were sucking noisily at their bottles of milk. This was Sister Charmaine's domain, four large, brightly painted rooms and a small one which contained incubators for the tiny, wizened little creatures struggling for life. Sister Charmaine, aged 38, had been presiding over these dormitories for 18 years. For someone who obviously slept on her feet, she looked remarkably young and fresh. I asked her how she managed to distinguish one baby – and its problems – from the next, for to me many babies looked alike.

'I remember all their names,' she said with a laugh. 'After all, I named them myself. These two are twins, and I know they have a Hindu mother. I have named them Sita and Gita, but because there should be no mistake, I have tagged Sita's name with a band on her wrist. These two are from Christian mothers; I have named them Martha and Mary. This one here, I call him Mithun,' she said pointing to a chuckling baby. 'He is such a handsome chap, maybe he'll also grow up to become a film star like Mithun Chakaravorty.'

By contrast, there was a little girl who looked very sickly. I asked the Sister about her. 'This one is Vaishali. Her mother had drugged herself a lot, but was unable to abort. Vaishali was born blind. Perhaps for this reason, she was left on the street. A couple passing by brought her to us. She was then only a month old. I took her to the hospital, where it was further diagnosed that she had a congenital heart disease. The hospital would not keep her without a full-time helper. I have nursed her these last four months. I feed her with a dropper a few drops at a time because she also has difficulty in swallowing. I believe that for each baby we get here, a hundred are aborted. Surely God has a special purpose for those whom he saves. I try not to lose these babies.'

Sister Charmaine continued her journey around the rooms. 'This one is Chamba, a premature girl. She is learning how to stand but she's a lazy baby. This one is Surya, such a happy boy, but see, he has a flat nose, so no one will adopt him. Here is Dimple. She was found in a strange way. A truck driver had stopped for lunch. When he got back into the truck, a street dog stood in front of the truck barking his head off. When the dog refused to budge, the driver became suspicious and clambered out. The dog led him to the side, where he found a newspaper bundle that was moving strangely. Inside he found this little child. She is so pretty and lively. God must have a special mission for her.'

I asked Sister Charmaine whether her work ever left her depressed. 'No,' she said, surprised by my question, 'this work is my life. The only thing I miss are my regular prayer times. But for me every baby here is God. God has given them life and I must help somehow to complete it, to let these children have a life through me.'

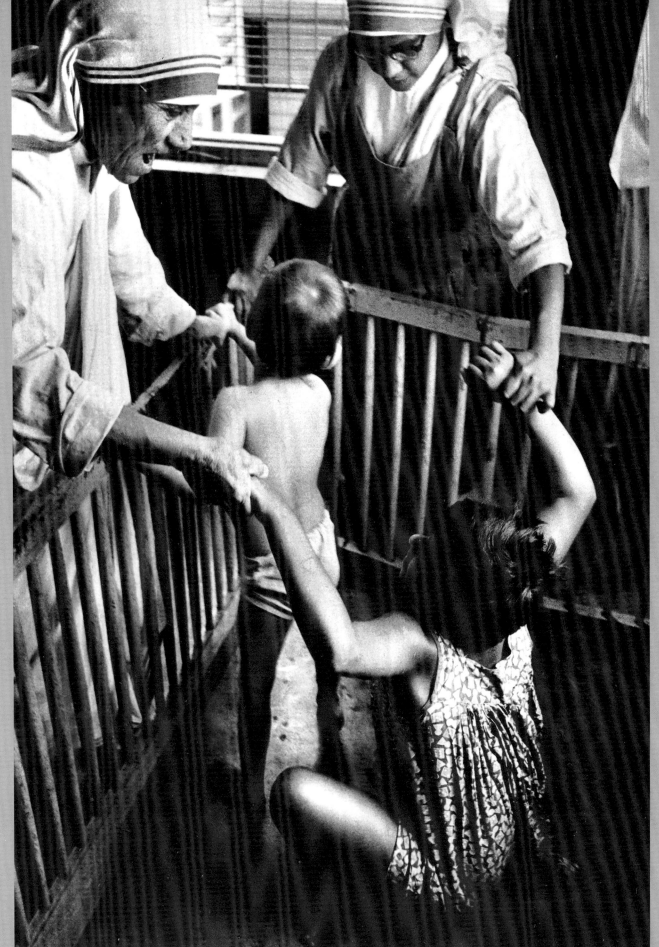

Mother Teresa and a Sister with children at Shishu Bhawan, Calcutta.

HOPE.

'A beautiful death'

For a Hindu, albeit not an especially practising one, I was brought up with the concept of death, rebirth and ultimate salvation, or *moksha*, where the soul is finally released from its relentless cosmic cycle into salvation. Suffering is viewed as the outcome of one's (mis)deeds in the previous life. Conversely, in the absence of suffering lay the fulfilment, in varying degrees of completeness, of one's *karma*, or duty. As an extension of this belief, the ailing body, therefore, was not as important as merit earned, for that would determine one's place in the next incarnation, unless one were to lead a life so perfect as to attain salvation and rest for eternity with the gods. However, I noticed on my visits to Kalighat that for Mother Teresa and her Sisters and Brothers, the 'broken bodies' of these total strangers were the focus of all existence, and on them they lavished not merely care but love.

I once asked Mother Teresa if, had she been allowed to retire in 1990, she would have preferred to spend her remaining days in Kalighat. She replied, not with any great conviction I felt, that it did not matter, since God was everywhere. Yet it is to these halls that I think she would have returned to pass the rest of her days. There is a small board here that proclaims this to be 'Mother's first love', which I believe to be the case. It is to these halls that Mother Teresa has brought those who have come to see her work – ordinary people and the rich and powerful. It is here that kings and presidents have been led and left feeling humbled by those they have encountered. Pope John Paul II has washed the feet of the wretched. American senators have stopped by in Calcutta with no purpose other than to lend a helping hand. Once when I accompanied Mother Teresa to Kalighat and saw a rich matron scrubbing the floor on her hands and knees, Mother Teresa remarked, 'I give them a chance to touch the poor, no? That is the beauty of God's work.'

When the municipality first offered her two halls adjoining the sacred Kali shrine, there was an uproar from the priests in the temple. There was local opposition and even threats. Angry young men periodically threw stones at the entrance of Nirmal Hriday. One day, when several stones hurtled through the windows, Mother Teresa stepped out to confront the group. With her hands outstretched, she approached the mob. 'Kill me if you want to,' she said, 'but do not disturb those inside. Let them die in peace.' For several long moments tension crackled in the air. Then a hush descended and the agitators turned away.

Mother Teresa has often said that many have died a 'beautiful death'. How can death be beautiful, I once asked? Naturally we feel lonely without a loved one, she had explained, but death meant 'going home'. She added, 'Those who die with us die in peace. For me that is the greatest development of human life, to die in peace and in dignity, for that is for eternity.'

'*A young girl wishing to join our Society must meet the four conditions that are required to become a Missionary of Charity. She must be healthy of mind and body. She must have the ability to learn. She must have plenty of common sense and a cheerful disposition.*'

'*It is not the excitement of the woman that draws our young Sisters. It is something much deeper. Many of our Sisters come from well-to-do families. To see them just leave their life behind is something wonderful. They are all anxious to live a life of poverty. To be able to understand the poor, to be able to understand the poverty of Christ, we choose to be poor. Many a time we freely choose not to have things we could easily have.*'

'*Keep smiling. Smile at Jesus in your suffering. For to be a real Missionary of Charity you must be a cheerful sufferer.*'

BODY OF CHRIST.

'*A girl came to join the Missionaries of Charity. We have a rule that the very next day new arrivals [in Calcutta] must go to the Home for the Dying. So I told this girl: "You saw Father during holy mass, with what love and care he touched Jesus in the host. Do the same when you go to the Home for the Dying, because it is the same Jesus you will find there in the broken bodies of our poor." After a few hours the newcomer came to me with a big smile — I have never seen a smile quite like that. I said to her: "What did you do?" She replied: "When we arrived there, they brought a man who had fallen into a drain, and had been there for some time. He was covered with wounds and dirt and maggots, and I cleaned him. For these hours I knew I was touching the body of Christ.*'*

MOTHER TERESA
in conversation with Navin Chawla

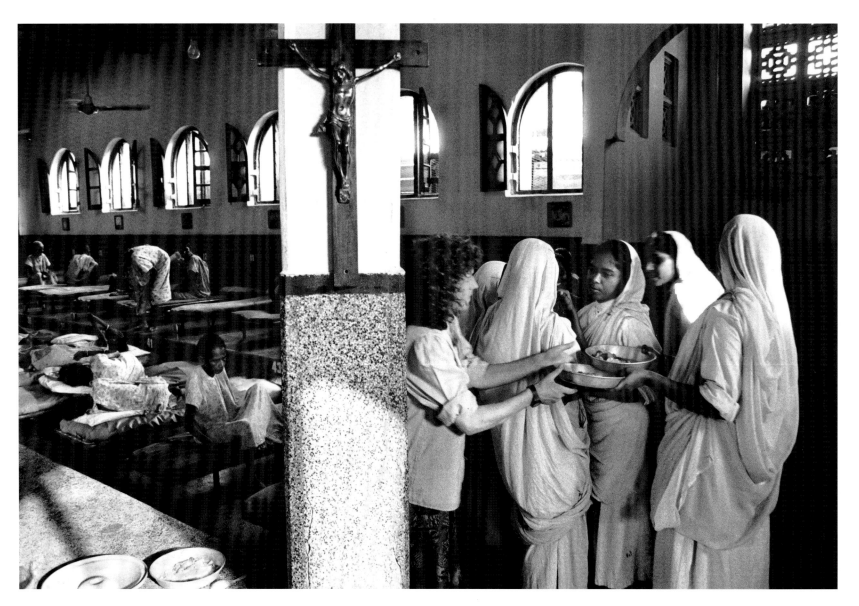

SISTERS, NOVICES AND A VOLUNTEER IN THE WOMEN'S WARD,

KALIGHAT, CALCUTTA.

Kalighat

I decided before I went to Calcutta that I would go and work at Kalighat, because this is where Mother Teresa sends novices on their first day. The ambulance which took me and the novices from Motherhouse sped through the teeming, incredibly noisy streets of Calcutta in the morning rush hour. Throughout the jolting bumpy ride the novices quietly prayed the rosary. Our progress slowed to almost walking pace as we neared Kalighat, and we drove along the busy market street lined with tiny open-fronted shops, in front of which squatted market women selling fruit, vegetables, garlands of flowers and colourful trinkets. The ambulance drew up at an open space in front of the temple alongside the rickshaws and yellow and black taxis; goats and dogs snuffled amongst the piles of market rubbish.

Kalighat means Kali's bank. The temple is near the river and is crowned with a silvered dome, and Mother Teresa's home for the dying destitutes lies in one corner of its complex; this has its own share of onion domes and was previously a rest house for pilgrims there.

You enter through brown double doors at the corner of the building and sometimes have to climb over groups of children or beggar women who sit waiting for left-over food, which is always brought to the door and distributed after each meal-time.

After the sunlight it is dark inside and the smell of disinfectant is at first overwhelming. Overwhelming too is the first sight of the men's ward, three rows of low metal beds. On them lie the pathetic wrecked bodies of the destitute of all ages.

The first morning after registering with Sister Suma, I helped the novices change the beds on the women's ward, and bathe the women. The first morning, whilst we had our tea-break on the roof, I was physically sick. Never had I seen anything like the twisted broken bodies of those women, or the stick-like limbs of the malnourished young people. Above the bleak, tiled shelf in the bath-house, are written the words 'the body of Christ' to remind us of the Sisters' vocation, and of our apostolate, to see our Lord in every human being, and especially in the poorest of the poor.

Though at first you are shocked by what you see at Kalighat, as you get to know the patients, very soon their dignity, their smiles and their appreciation change you, and you realize that this seemingly bleak, impoverished place is an expression of God's love. 'Whatsoever you did to the least of these my children, you did it to me.'

Many of the women at Kalighat when I was there were mentally disturbed. They would lie or sit with a hand permanently outstretched begging. Some had been so long on the streets that they preferred to sleep on the ground; even the hard metal bed with the thin mattress filled with coconut fibre was spurned. Many of the mattresses were made from the white sacks we sent the clothing to India in. No one is ever turned away from Kalighat, so if there was no bed, a mattress would go on the floor.

One day on my way to Kalighat I noticed a woman lying on the narrow concrete division in the centre of a dual carriageway in the hot sun. I told Sister Suma, and as there was no ambulance available, we went back in a taxi to find her. When the taxi driver asked Sister what sort of a patient we were going to fetch, she gave the simple answer: your sister. The woman was not as ill as she had at first seemed and decided she did not wish to stay, but returned to beg on the streets after a bath and a meal.

Others came in by ambulance, having been found by the Sisters or Brothers who patrol the streets, particularly near Howrah and Sealdah Stations, where many of the destitute land up. One such was Bobita, in her late teens. She was brought in by Brother Das, who found her huddled on the pavement shaking with fever, crawling with lice, and crippled from having been so long squatting and begging on the streets. She very nearly didn't survive those first few days, but when I was there she had been at Kalighat for several months, and was well on the way to recovery. Besides being unable to walk, she was profoundly deaf. Her sunny personality and teasing nature made her a great favourite. I asked Sister Suma what would happen to her, and Sister said that she would be found a place helping in a kitchen at one of the homes. Bobita would never suffer destitution on the streets again.

The morning routine is to finish clearing the breakfast. Then the changing of the beds and the bathing of the patients begins. Many are crippled and have to be carried. Others shuffle along, crouched down. Priobla, who was blind, would progress to the bath with her arms round the waist of a novice or a volunteer. Whilst some novices and volunteers were helping the bathing, others were disinfecting and changing all the beds, and washing the floor. Everyone was bathed and given a new nightie.

The washing of all the sheets, nighties and pyjamas of over 100 ill and sometimes doubly incontinent people was done in the central area between the men's and women's wards. A dhobi wallah, or Indian washerman, did the morning washing aided by volunteers, who then carried the washing up to the roof, where it was hung up to dry. Every second Thursday, the furnace in the washing area was lit, and all the bed-linen and nighties etc. were boiled up. Eight or ten of us would stand round and slap the steaming sheets in unison on the flat concrete, making a noise like thunder, accompanied by much laughter if someone got out of time.

At 10.30 every morning whilst the novices were giving out the medicines, the volunteers gathered on the roof for tea, and a welcome break in the fresh air. This was a time to discuss with colleagues what you had seen and done, and to get to know new volunteers. These volunteers come from a dozen different countries in Europe, as well as South America, Asia and Japan. Many from Poland and East Germany were travelling abroad for the first time. Mother Teresa has made Calcutta into a place of pilgrimage.

On the roof of Kalighat, at one corner, a statue of Our Lady of Fatima looks out over the teeming streets of the city. In a simple building at the top of the stairs is a chapel bare of all furniture except the altar, above which is the crucifix and the words 'I THIRST'; a place of peace, a place of prayer.

One day Sister asked me to go to each woman patient and to mark either their bangles or rings, or some other sign of identification, down in the registration book. This was to help at medicine time, because although the beds were numbered, many of the patients were mentally handicapped and would swap beds in the night; they might then be given the wrong medication.

Sister Suma showed me the first registers of Kalighat, and they were, for the first two years, all written in Mother's hand. The first patient came to Kalighat in August 1952. He lived for only 12 hours. At that time Kalighat was supported by the gifts of local people whom the nuns had begged from. Now they still beg at Christmas time, so it will never lose its aspect of being the house of the poorest of the poor. When you are there, most surely you see the crucified Christ in the broken emaciated bodies of those you care for. But you also see Christ smiling through the smiles and eyes of those you care for — indeed: 'Make us worthy Lord to serve our fellow men who live and die in poverty and hunger.'

MARY COX
co-worker, Sussex, UK

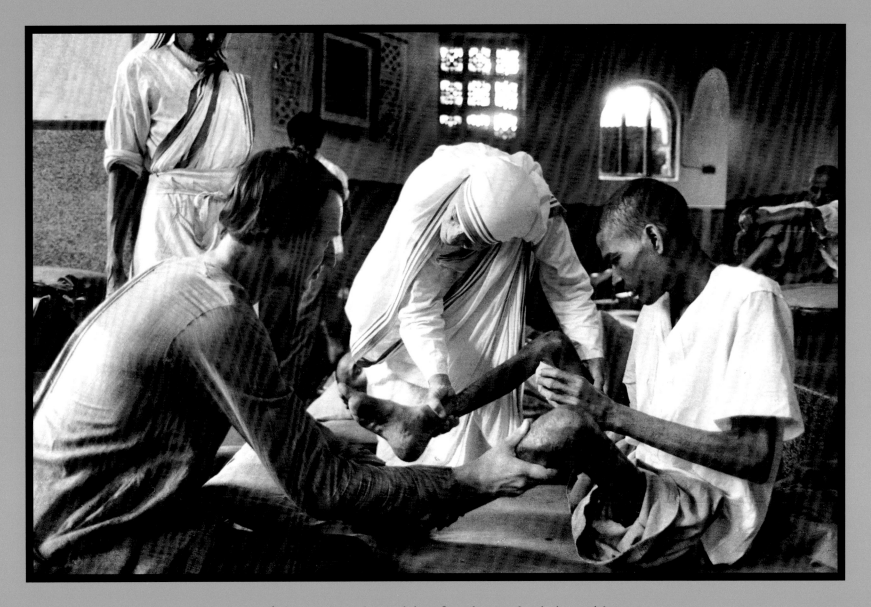

'*There is always the possibility of people going [to the hospitals].*
But who is there for those falling beside the way? Somebody has to be there for them.'
SISTER ANDREA

My career in nursing started in a hospital in the East End of London during the Second World War. It continued in hospitals in Exeter and Edinburgh and abroad in Uganda. After obtaining a BA degree and many years spent in teaching, it was time to retire. My husband had died and my children were grown up. Quite suddenly I decided to go to Calcutta with the intention of working as a volunteer with Mother Teresa.

During my first visit of three months, and a later visit of the same length, I worked in Shishu Bhawan, Kalighat, Prem Dan and for a month at the leprosarium Shanti-Nagar near Asansol.

Being present in the Motherhouse when Mother Teresa was at home, and at mass and adoration, gave us great happiness. Sometimes she would talk to us and bless us as we put on our sandals, or maybe give us a miraculous medal for a sick relative or friend. Sometimes it seemed so little we could do, but Mother said just being there was important.

One of my lasting impressions of all the establishments of the Sisters was the hard work entailed in keeping everywhere clean; perhaps not the ultra-hygienic standards we are used to, but every use was made of the help and resources available. The wards were washed from top to bottom every week and everything moveable cleaned and aired in the sun. Washing and drying the linen kept us all busy in some of the compounds. The patients, too, were kept bathed and clean. Food was served with great care and there always seemed plenty to go round. Stainless steel goblets and plates were scrubbed with detergent and remained shining and indestructible. (I wondered if washing machines or dishwashers would ever be installed.) Attention to the basic rules of hygiene helped to prevent cross-infection, especially with babies and children; quite a difficult problem when facilities for even hand-washing are restricted. Nevertheless supervision of the preparation of the infants' feeding bottles was good and so vital for their well-being.

Sometimes patients had wounds requiring skilled care. Either the Sisters or the volunteers always provided medical help and resources to meet the need. One day a young woman was brought into Kalighat in a state of shock and with severe lacerations to her foot and lower leg. A car had run over her as she sat on the ground. For some reason she could not be admitted to hospital, but in Kalighat she received good medical treatment and her pain was kept under control. When I left she was well on the way to recovery. The patients all welcomed a friendly hug and especially enjoyed having oil rubbed into their hair. Language, or rather lack of it, seemed not to matter. The babies and children were cuddled and played with. Perhaps one day there will be more facilities.

Meeting volunteers of all ages and from so many different countries was an unexpected pleasure: there were all religions and none, highly qualified professional people, and those with no special skills at all but with one desire to help and love others. Apart from real and lasting friendships, there was always a readiness to share knowledge and to give and receive help from each other. Calcutta was fascinating. Even the noise, pollution, dust and poverty were balanced by the vibrant, colourful and exciting scenes of everyday life. Certainly a city of contrasts.

One night the Sisters and volunteers spent many hours helping to unload a fleet of container lorries. These were parked on the main road and the goods carried by a human chain to be stored in the depths of Shishu Bhawan. This particular load came from Europe and included large and heavy tins of special high-protein nutritious biscuits, dried milk and bales of clothing.

There are times when the news, international and national, moves one to despair. I just think of Mother Teresa and the Sisters and remember that, although what we do to help may be very little, yet that little bit matters, wherever we may be, especially if it's done with a smile and love.

No doubt the needs will change. Social problems of alcoholism, drug abuse and the spread of Aids will have devastating effects. God willing, there will always be people who care and are able to bring relief and hope to the poorest of the poor.

EILEEN MANLEY
co-worker, Lechlade, Gloucestershire, UK

Hasina

As I walked past bed number 26, its occupant sat up with a strength that belied her frail frame. Hasina, for that was her name, reached out for the Sister's hand and pulled her close so that she could whisper in her ear. She spoke in Bengali, at first slowly and then, as if she had recovered her confidence, in great bursts. She laughed and cried alternatively. She had been a beggar on Ripon Street and had a perch that she had occupied almost every day without a break for many years. It was under a large shady tree that protected her from the sun and gave shelter from the rain; it stood at a busy intersection where a number of buses halted. Commuters boarded or changed here. Hasina was a favourite among the regulars; she was an old woman with a kindly smile and never forgot to exchange a few words with them. By 6pm or a little later, when most passengers had made their way home, her little aluminium bowl had filled up quite nicely. On a good day she could make as much as ten rupees. Then disaster struck. A series of violent strikes paralysed the city. An order banned gatherings of more than five people. Everyday life was affected and most people stayed away from work. After a few days of this, Hasina set off for her post but found herself unable to get there. It was over a week before the city lurched back to normal, and Hasina was able to return to her station. To her dismay she found that her spot had been taken over by an entire family, who had spread themselves liberally across the site. Frantically, she tried other corners but they were either someone else's 'property' or less strategically placed. She tried a few other locations, but nothing worked and she simply had no energy left to go further afield to more distant spots. Her anxiety was compounded by her family's disappointment at her dwindling contribution. When they realized that she was now without income, they closed the doors on

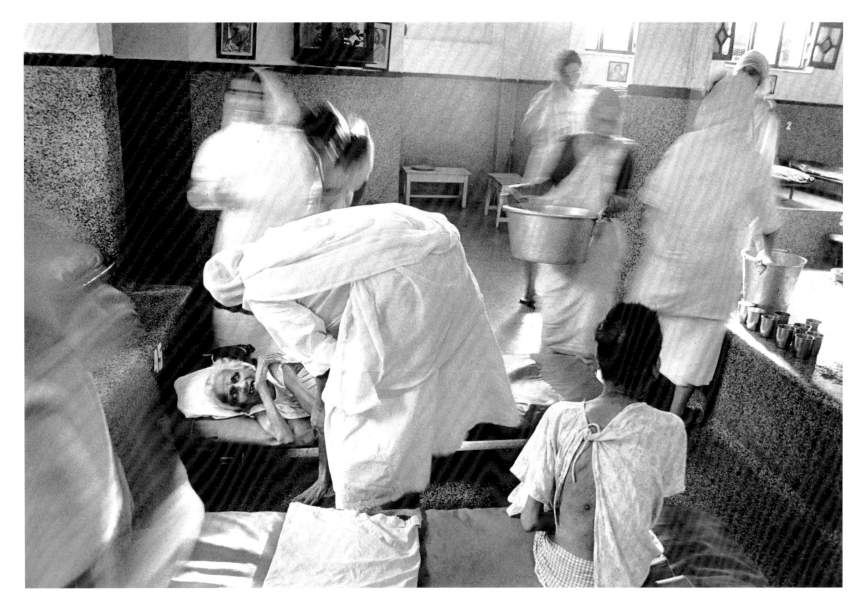

HASINA.

her. The Sisters found her lying on Ripon Street. She was dying. They carried her to Nirmal Hriday and nursed her. She was force-fed for ten days before she recovered. No sooner had she done so than she begged the Sisters to inform her family. They did so. No one came. Now Hasina lies quietly, clinging to her aluminium bowl. Her eyes are invariably on the door, in the hope that one day someone will take her home.

NAVIN CHAWLA
in Kalighat

Shanti Dān

'Have you ever been to Tengra?' Mother Teresa asked me one morning in Calcutta. 'The Government asked me to take care of mentally handicapped girls who were in the jails. I said I would take them all but I needed space. So the Government gave me sixteen acres of land at the price of one rupee a year, just imagine, and I put up the buildings. It is very beautiful work, go and see it.'

As soon as we entered the district of Tengra I stopped to ask for directions. No one seemed to know where Shanti Dān (Gift of Peace home) was. 'Mother Teresa's home,' I said. 'Oh, Mother Teresa' came a chorus in unison and several hands pointed in the general direction of a large walled complex. Here I met Sister Bella. I asked if I could look around. The building, I noticed, was a spanking new one that contained three dormitories on each of its two floors. I had long since got used to seeing spotless floors in Mother Teresa's institutions, but here there was an almost luxurious quality about the way everything had been arranged. The rooms themselves were bright and airy with ceiling fans and each bed had its mosquito net. Colourful chequered bedlinen had been woven by the leprosy patients in Titagarh. Not a pin seemed out of place. There was no sign of volunteers or paid workers. I gathered that Mother Teresa did not permit them to help here, because the patients were encouraged to keep themselves and their environment clean as a necessary part of occupational therapy. As I passed groups of patients I expected to encounter anger or hostility. Instead they greeted me with warm *namastes* and many waved to me.

'When they came here two years ago they would not put on their clothes. They could not eat properly. When we tried to go near them, they would cower with fear in a corner. Now they do most things for themselves. Some of these women have been in jail wards for years on end. We have come very far in this time. It is only when they are really sick or feeling low that they go inside to lie down during the day, otherwise they sit in or tend the gardens, or do simple work in the crafts centre. See these dolls here,' said Sister, pointing to some neatly handcrafted items on a shelf, 'these are done by some of these girls.' I noticed some little handmade bags, one on every bed, and asked what they were. 'School bags,' said the Sister with a laugh. 'A benefactor donated all of them along with some books – alphabets and simple story books – and items of stationery. Soon teachers volunteered to give lessons and now they really look forward to their classes. Small things make them so happy!'

Several years ago I headed the health department of Delhi state. In the course of administering a dozen large hospitals I visited the female ward of a hospital for mentally disturbed patients. One of my most vivid memories remains the ward where severely mentally disabled women were locked in. Some of them were sedated, but in spite of this they habitually tore at their hair, their clothes, their blankets. Their condition was one of the most saddening scenes that I can recall. Now, as I went around the wooded complex at Shanti Dān and saw what may have been the same people sitting by the wooded lake silent and at peace, I realized what the philosophy of love in action meant, and that a simple woman's faith had wrought this miracle out of nothingness.

SMALL THINGS MAKE THEM SO HAPPY.

DALIM DAS.

It was early evening by the time Sister Suma led me to the women's hall. Little had changed since my last visit, and yet, in a sense, everything had. When I was last here I had spent time talking with Dalim Das, once a governess with a wealthy family. Dalim was dying of cancer. The disease appeared to have invaded her entire body. She had lost her hair, probably the after-effects of chemotherapy. Sister whispered to me that sometimes her pain was so intense, she screamed for the end to come. Yet all the time that she spoke with me, she never made a sound nor expressed any sadness or regret. Her 'indisposition' might have been a slight headache that would go away soon. I was, after all, a stranger, and well-bred ex-governesses did not discuss their ailments in public. She spoke about the years gone by, when she accompanied her wards to Europe, and that made me forget that we were in the Home of the Dying. We might instead have been sipping tea at the Grand Hotel in Chowringhee Street. It was only as our conversation drew to an end, and we both realized that we were unlikely to meet again, that she made a personal admission. She told me that she had fought her cancer for nine years armed only with willpower and prayer; she was a Hindu, but she prayed not only to the vast pantheon of Hindu gods and goddesses, but to Jesus Christ and Allah besides. For the end of her litany, Dalim reserved a very special prayer, one that she herself composed. It was a little prayer to Mother Teresa. She prayed for her moksha, her salvation, that she might be spared the cycle of birth and death, with all the pain that accompanied life, and go home finally to God. Sometimes this prayer would assume form and substance, and Dalim Das would find Mother Teresa herself sitting by her side, holding her hand or stroking her brow.

NAVIN CHAWLA
Mother Teresa, *Sinclair-Stevenson, London, 1992*

Calendar art on a Calcutta
street. Mother Teresa amongst
pictures of Hindu Gods and
Goddesses and film stars.

'THE PEOPLE of Calcutta give, even without anyone asking,' said Mother Teresa in her abbreviated manner of speaking. 'Whenever something is needed, people just come and give whatever they can. This happens with our Sisters every single day.' No sooner had she said this to me than she saw someone standing near the top of the stairs by the chapel door. 'Excuse me for a minute,' she said and got up to meet the newcomer. I turned around. I saw a well-dressed Bengali lady, looking rather hesitant about approaching Mother Teresa. It was clear she had never met Mother Teresa before. Mother Teresa held her hands and then blessed her. The woman burst into tears. Through her sobs I could hear her say she had brought a small offering for the poor. Beside her were two large bags of rice. I can testify that they were indeed very heavy, because on Mother's bidding, I carried them down to the parlour, from where they would be despatched to Shishu Bhawan, where the needy were fed each morning.

A POSTER PAINTED BY CHILDREN, SHISHU BHAWAN, CALCUTTA.

To be alone or together for God in silence. There it is that we accumulate the inward power which we distribute in action, put in the smallest duty and spend in the severest hardships that befall us.

Silence came before creation, and the heavens were spread without a word.

Christ was born in the dead of night; and though there has been no power like his, 'He did not strive nor cry, neither was his voice heard in the streets.'

Once I was asked by someone what I consider most important in the training of the Sisters. I answered: 'Silence. Interior and exterior silence. Silence is essential in a religious house. The silence of humility and of charity, the silence of the eye, of the ears, of the tongue. There is no life of prayer without silence. Silence, and then kindness, charity; silence leads to charity, charity to humility. Charity among themselves, accepting one another when they are different; charity for union in a community. Charity leads to humility. We must be humble, like God. He humbles himself. Even today He shows His humility by making use of instruments as deficient as we are, weak, imperfect, inadequate instruments.'

From My Life for the Poor – Mother Teresa of Calcutta,
edited by José Luis Gonzalez-Balado and Janet N Playfoot,
Ballantine Books, New York, 1975

'In the morning, we have a full hour of silence. When we work we don't talk unless it is necessary.

Wherever you go, you will observe perfect silence as we go about our work.

For it is in the silence of the heart that God speaks.'

MOTHER TERESA
in conversation with Navin Chawla, 25 March 1996, Calcutta

'*We do no great things, only
small things with great love.*'
MOTHER TERESA

L.D.M.

MISSIONARIES OF CHARITY
54A ACHARYA J. CHANDRA BOSE
CALCUTTA 700016, INDIA

30/8/93

My dearest Co-workers,

Thank you for your prayers and concern for my health. Thank God I am really better now and at home in the Mother House.

I had wanted to bring all of you to Calcutta for a chapter to tell you what is in my heart regarding the Co-workers. Now is not possible.

May God's blessing be with you all and help you to accept my decision which I have made after much prayer and penance and suffering

I am very grateful for all the wonderful work each one of you has done right from the beginning. These 25 years have been something beautiful for God. I want to thank you especially those who were with me from the beginning specially Mrs Ann Blaikie Jesus said - "You did it to Me" Your reward will be great in Heaven.

Dear Co-Workers, to keep up your spirit as Co-workers, you need only remain in close touch with the Missionaries of Charity and among yourselves wherever you are. I want you to work with

2

MISSIONARIES OF CHARITY
54A ACHARYA J. CHANDRA BOSE
CALCUTTA 700016, INDIA

the Sisters, Brothers and Fathers directly - the humble work, beginning in your own homes, neighbourhood your parish, your city; and where there are no Missionaries of Charity, to work in that same spirit wherever you may be. It is this that will transform the world. If you pray, God will give a clean heart and a clean heart can see the Face of God in the Poor you serve. Now that times have changed and Sisters are in 105 countries of the World, we do not need the Co-workers to function as an "Organization" with Governing Board, Officers, links and bank accounts. I do not want money to be spent for newsletters, or for travel as Co-workers. If you see anyone raising money in my name please stop them. And any money offered to you for Mother Teresa or the Missionaries of Charity must be directed immediately and entirely to the Missionaries of Charity. As long as you observe these points, you belong to the family of the Missionaries of Charity and can be Co workers of Mother Teresa. However, I do not want

'Conversion is not our work — that is the work of God. We never ask anyone to change their religion. Our mission is to reveal God by doing our service.'

<small>MOTHER TERESA TO NAVIN CHAWLA</small>

3.

MISSIONARIES OF CHARITY
54A ACHARYA J. CHANDRA BOSE
CALCUTTA 700016, INDIA

the Co-workers as an "organization"
to continue. I have written to all
the Bishops around the world that
I have made this decision.

Let us all remain united in
the Heart of Jesus through Mary
as one spiritual family. My gift
to you is to allow you to share
with us in God's work, to be
carriers of God's love in a spirit
of prayer and sacrifice.
I appeal to you once more - be
what Mother is asking you to be,
in each city and town - simple
Co-workers, helping the Sisters to
bring Jesus to the Poor. I send
my special blessing and deep
gratitude for doing as I ask you.
Let us all be one heart full of
love in the Heart of Jesus full
of love for Mary and through the
Immaculate Heart of Mary. The
cause of our joy
Let us often say - Mary Mother of
Jesus be Mother to us now.
Each one of you are in my
daily. Let us be one heart full of love
Let us pray   God bless you
                            M Teresa mc

*MOTHER TERESA WITH A GROUP
OF BROTHERS OF THE
MISSIONARIES OF CHARITY.*

15th March 53

LDM.

My dear Sister

Your two letters of Feb
have been on my table
and as much as I would have liked
to write to you. I could not.

We have at last come to our convent
I am sure you are longing to see it - as
soon as somebody takes a photo I shall
send you one -

I did not write to you - but my thoughts
are very often with you & when things are
difficult - my _____ has encouraged with the
thought of having you to pray & suffer for me
then I find it easy & the smile for the good God
comes much quicker. - It must be so hard
for you to write - & yet you do it - I need
all that you can give - I am really very
happy to have you - it is one of the
big big grace God has given me - to have
given you to me - The Sisters feel
the same for their Sisters - Just now
cannot write - as they are

preparing for their profession. The
first 10 - will be professed on the
12th April - They will make their
Vows for one year - I will make
my final Vows on the same day -
So my Sister Jacqueline will be
at the altar with me also
As for the medicines you can
Send - but there will be some
Jesuit Father coming home so
when they come back you could
send through them

Spiritual books will be most
welcome - I am very particular
about having good books for my
Sisters - so if you chance
to get any - I shall be very grateful
I would like you to say some
of our simple prayers we say -
So that you could be more
united - At present I cannot

*MOTHER TERESA BLESSES A
VISITOR AT THE ENTRANCE TO THE
HOME FOR THE DYING, KALIGHAT.*

Get them printed – but as soon as
the Sisters finish the copy I shall send it
to you. May be some generous person
would do that for us in Belgium.
For everything we depend on Divine
Providence and it is wonderful what
tender care He takes of us – just because
we cling to Poverty.
Please tell Mrs. Thomson, Miss Marguerite
Miss Joan & Miss Winifred that I accept
them with my whole heart as spiritual
Members. and that we depend much
on them for the work in the missions.
Dear Sister. Take care of yourself – I
wish I could take a little from your
terrible suffering – but you see a
Missionary of Charity has to be a burning
fire' & that is what the Good God is
making of you. Agnes & Nicholas send
you their love – they pray for me. I feel
so strong with the three of you – Thank
God for giving me you, Agnes
& Nicholas, Mrs Thomson, Marguerite Winifred
Joan and the 28 Sisters. Yours in Jesus
M Teresa

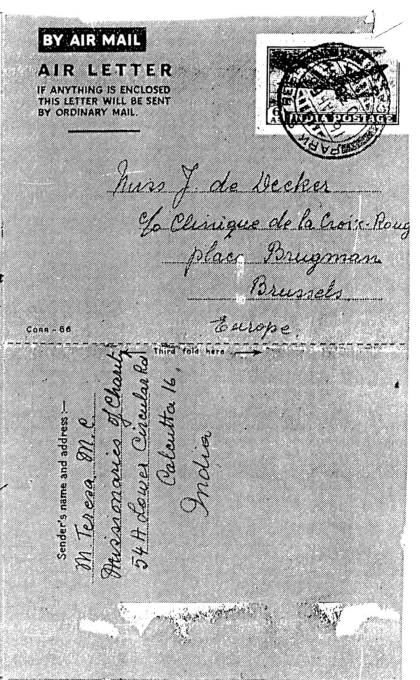

BY AIR MAIL

AIR LETTER

IF ANYTHING IS ENCLOSED
THIS LETTER WILL BE SENT
BY ORDINARY MAIL.

CORR - 66

Miss J. de Decker
c/o Clinique de la Croix-Roug
place Brugman
Brussels
Europe

Third fold here

Sender's name and address :-
M Teresa. M. C.
Missionaries of Charity
54 A Lower Circular Rd
Calcutta 16,
India

MOTHER TERESA BLESSES A SISTER BEFORE

SHE EMBARKS ON AN OVERSEAS TOUR.

Toshi Fumi Tawarayama, aged 22 from Kanagawa, Japan, belongs to a Buddhist family, but he confessed he was not himself especially religious. When I saw him in Kalighat he was wearing a red scarf around his head and a smile on his face. He told me that after he finished high school, he took on a variety of jobs in Japan and later in Canada. I asked him what work he did in Kalighat. He said he washed blankets. 'Not many people want to wash blankets. I prefer to talk to patients and help them, but it is important to wash blankets too,' he said. 'It's a choice we have. I get more joy in giving with my hands and heart.' How had he heard about Mother Teresa, I asked? He had seen a documentary on the work of the Missionaries of Charity in Japan some years ago, which had stirred him, but when he first saw Mother Teresa in Kalighat, going from patient to patient, he came close to tears. 'We [in Japan] may be materially rich, but we are not so mentally rich.' Then he added, 'I will not forget.'

NAVIN CHAWLA
in conversation with Toshi Fumi Tawarayama

'I had heard of Mother Teresa while I was in school. I had read her sayings and a little of her life. I had thought of coming to Calcutta as a volunteer, but when a friend of mine was here last year [from Germany] and came back and told me everything, I decided to come. He told me everything realistically – the problems of traffic, noise and diseases, but he loved Kalighat and Prem Dan. I felt at peace to do it.'

'I have been here for three months. The patients give you a lot of love back. I say to God, take these people and keep them happy in the other life. I believe He hears me.'

'I have developed a special bond with one woman here. You would not look at her in the street. She is blind, but there is much love in her. She speaks to me in Bengali and also knows a few words of English. "Darling", "Cheerio", "Bye-Bye", she often says. She is like a little child to me. When I take her in my arms, both she and I are happy. When she learned I am to leave, all she could say was "No go", "No go".'

'The Sisters reflect a very special charisma from Mother Teresa. The volunteers are included in their faith and love. It's a circle of peace. I have seen people come from hospitals and get saved by the love and care they receive from the Sisters and volunteers, for healing is not the only answer. In Germany I work in a hospital. Many nurses tell me that they don't have enough time for patients. In Kalighat I have received a gift from God. I have met beautiful people. In Germany I will try to do this work in a stronger way, but I will come back here again.'

ANGELIKA KÖNIG
Freiburg, Germany

'I read about Mother Teresa in a book and it became a dream to go to Calcutta. I then volunteered to work a month in a summer camp run by the Missionaries of Charity in London. Here I met a number of volunteers who had been to Calcutta, many much younger than me. Their lives touched me. When I came to Calcutta, I had never seen such poverty before. I visited Shishu Bhawan and Kalighat, before asking the Sisters if I could work in Kalighat.'

'Mother Teresa enjoins us to "try to do very small things with great love". The people here in Kalighat realize that death is not the end but a beginning. The poor help us to realise so much about human respect and dignity. There is a lot of kindness amongst each other. We are not the givers, we are the recipients.'

TANIA STACKHOUSE
Hereford, UK

Accounts on pp 168–170 recounted by volunteers to Navin Chawla in Kalighat, 23 March 1996

*Talking to a visitor on
the bridge leading to
her small office,
Motherhouse, Calcutta.*

Why did you choose India? And of all places in India, why this hell-hole Calcutta?' She let a gentle smile come over her face. 'India was a missionary country, I was sent here. And I love the people of Calcutta. They have a warmth which you don't see anywhere else.' She told me of an experience which made the people of Calcutta so lovable. 'During the floods last year I was bringing victims to places of shelter. A lady who had never known me brought me hot food in her car. Where else in the world do you come across people like that?' It is obvious that Mother Teresa would have gone to any country to which she was sent, with the same unquestioning obedience, and worked up the same enthusiasm for the people amongst whom she had to live. Since she was sent to India, she assiduously Indianized herself. Hers was the first Catholic order to adopt the Indian sari, the Indian style of squatting cross-legged on the floor in the chapel, eating Indian food in the Indian manner. She taught herself Bengali, which she now speaks fluently and, when India became free, she took Indian nationality. Mother Teresa's strength to do what she does comes from simple convictions. ('She is blessed with certainties,' wrote Muggeridge.) When I asked her, 'Who has been the dominant influence in your life? Gandhi, Nehru, Schweitzer?' without even a pause to ponder over my question, she replied, 'Jesus Christ.'

'What about books? Have you read anything that you consider having influenced your thinking?'

'The scriptures.'

REACHING OUT TO HER APOSTOLATE.

I changed the subject and asked her how she got the money to run her world-wide organization. She replied: 'It comes, money is no great problem. God gives through His people. We have never been short of money. It is more important to get people involved, to make them realize that the sick, old and hungry are their brothers, no? When you write about me, I hope you will capitalize that.' When she started her first school in the slums, all she had was five rupees. But as people came to know what she was doing, they brought things and money. 'It was all divine providence,' she said and narrated some miracles. Once in winter-time they ran out of quilts. The nuns found sheets but there was no cotton to stuff in them. Mother Teresa got her pillow and just as she was about to rip it open the bell rang. Somebody who was leaving Calcutta for a posting abroad had come to leave his quilts and mattresses with Mother Teresa. On another occasion when they had run out of rice, a lady who had never been to them before brought a bag of rice. Out of curiosity they measured the amount with the tin cup they used for measuring their daily rations. It happened to be exactly the quantity they required. 'When I told the lady that, she broke down and cried… to realize that God had used her as an instrument of His will was too much for her.'

That afternoon I was with Mother Teresa on a 'begging mission'. We went to call on the manager of a big biscuit factory. 'They always give us broken biscuits they cannot sell, as a Christmas gift. The sick like broken biscuits,' she informed me. Mr Jyoti Mukerjee, the young manager of the firm, came out to receive her and escorted us to his teak-wood-panelled, air-conditioned office. Mother Teresa began by thanking him for what he had done in the past and continued, 'You must have lots of problems. Everything is in short supply: flour, butter, sugar, no?' It was evident that Mr Mukerjee's speech had been taken out of his mouth. 'Yes,' he agreed, 'we are not producing anything like we did last year.'

Mother Teresa went on: 'It must be more difficult for well-to-do people of the middle class. We poor people can beg, they are too ashamed to beg, no?' I could see Mr Mukerjee's defences crumble. He looked unhappy with himself. Mother Teresa continued in a gentler tone. 'Why are all these shortages? Why are prices going up? Please tell me. I do not understand politics.' Jyoti Mukerjee became expansive and told her of union troubles, strikes and lock-outs. 'Thank God!' exclaimed Mother Teresa. 'We only work for God; there are no unions.' She proceeded to elucidate on the hard times. 'The other day we picked up a hungry beggar. He had not eaten for many weeks. When we brought him a plate of rice he said, "I haven't seen rice for many weeks; let me look at it!" And he died staring at that plateful of rice.' Mr Mukerjee picked up his phone and rang up the store-keeper for 40 large tins of broken biscuits to be delivered to Mother Teresa.

KHUSHWANT SINGH
Gurus, Godmen and Good People, *Orient Longman, Bombay, 1975*

IT IS ON the bridge that connects the chapel to her small office room that Mother Teresa meets the many hundreds of people who come to see her each week. After her heart ailment in 1989, doctors tried to restrict her activities, without much success. The only concession she seemingly made was that she saw fewer people in the parlour downstairs, which certainly reduced the number of times she climbed up and down the stairs each day. For years, she has been Calcutta's foremost tourist attraction, far outpacing the Victoria Memorial and the other relics of the British Raj that dot the city. More often than not, tourists arrive by the busload and the queue they form snakes its way from the entrance of Motherhouse, past the Virgin in the Grotto, through the courtyard and up the stairs. A few times I have seen an empty courtyard suddenly fill until there is no standing room. On these occasions, Mother Teresa has simply blessed the assemblage from the bridge.

On more normal days she meets everyone with undivided attention, even if it is for only half a minute. Each person is given a printed prayer ('my business card,' she jokes, her face wreathed in smiles) or a medallion of the Virgin ('Wear it, it works miracles,' she says). Some want a few words with her and they clutch her hands as they whisper. Others ask her whether they can have a picture taken with her, not a prospect she much enjoys, but she does not refuse as long as it does not become too repetitive. I have seen people who, meeting her for the first time, are so overcome with emotion that they burst into tears. When this happens, she invariably holds their head with both her hands and comforts them. Many have told me that their meeting with her, however brief, is one they are unlikely ever to forget.

The people (apart from her own Sisters) who meet her most often are the volunteers. Of all ages and nationalities, some travel to Calcutta after years of prevarication, while others stumble upon the Missionaries of Charity almost by accident during their tours of India. Once they start work, they quickly fall into the routine. Although not obliged to attend mass or adoration, most do, irrespective of their faith or lack of it. After prayers, they manage to have Mother Teresa to themselves for a quiet interchange.

I have often seen groups of volunteers in the chapel at Motherhouse, sometimes 30 or 40 sitting together on one side of the chapel floor. Most of them have donned the Indian *kurta* pyjama, a loose cotton outfit that enables them to move and work more comfortably, while remaining relatively cool. After mass they head for duties assigned to them by the Sisters, where they remain the whole day.

In Calcutta, where the largest group of volunteers invariably is, they fan out to Shishu Bhawan, Prem Dan, the Nirmala Kennedy Centre and Kalighat. Their duties, assigned by the Sister in charge, may vary. The medically qualified find their work cut and dried for them. Others may be sent to look after children, to wash linen, clean floors or disinfect rooms. They may simply be called upon to sit with the sick and comfort them. In doing so, they are able to overcome linguistic barriers by the universal language of humanism.

To have come from another world to provide succour to the poorest of the poor – was this their *bhagya*, their fate?

I asked this of Eamon Butler, a young carpenter from Ireland. 'This is a question I have asked myself every day for the past six weeks,' he replied. 'I could be home in Ireland enjoying a social life with the money I make.' For several minutes I had watched him make an old man more comfortable. He had given him a shave and changed his bedclothes. The man then soiled his

WITH A VOLUNTEER ON THE BRIDGE.

bed and Butler cleaned him again. 'When I arrived in Motherhouse I was asked to work in Kalighat. A shiver went down my spine. Sister asked me to go for a half a day and see,' he added.

After a pause, he continued, 'As soon as I walked in, I felt a special grace, which has helped me to cope with what I saw. Within a week I was able to hold dying people, wash the dead, something I could never have dreamed of. Now I have seen death in a different light – as a rebirth, as life after; as the "final stuff". The body goes, the soul and peace remain. I have found myself at peace with death. And I have seen some wonderful things about life as well. How human beings are, how people in the streets care for one another, the way they care here in Kalighat, and the love of the Sisters. The frustration for a lot of us is to return to a world full of materialism. I say to myself that I will allow the pain and suffering to penetrate me so deeply that I will want to change.'

MOTHER TERESA's first two companions were Subhasini Das, who took Mother Teresa's own name of Agnes, and Magdalena Gomes, who became Sister Gertrude. They joined within a week of each other. On 19 March 1949, Mother Teresa wrote in her book, 'A great day. Subhasini Das joined the little Society. We went to Baithak Khana for her consecration to our Lady. May the Immaculate Heart, Cause of our Joy, guide and help, bless and protect the beginnings of this her least Society. She is beautifully simple. God keep her like this.' And on 26 March, Mother Teresa wrote 'Great day – Magdalena (Gomes) joined the little Society. She is a fine strong soul. She will just do well with the poor. She must smile down on us, trying to give our Queen all our love and devotion.'

Almost 50 years later, the memories of the earliest days were vividly recalled by Sister Gertrude. I asked her of her family's reaction to the prospect of her joining Mother Teresa, at a time when Mother Teresa and her fledgling society were completely unknown. She admitted that her father was horrified. He had already lost his son in an accident. Now his only daughter had donned a sari of the kind worn in those days by the lowest caste of sweepers, and had stepped into the streets. 'He wrote to me,' she recalled, '"God took away my son. This I can bear. But I cannot bear to see you in the slums and have people talk against you." For two years, he often saw me, but he never spoke to me.' But for me, from the very start, it was a challenge. I knew we could not go to the poor in Western dress. They would have called us *mem-sahib* and shut the door on us. We had to do, as Mother said, what Jesus did. Jesus became a poor man. We would not have been approachable if we did not step out in poverty.

I asked her whether she had been studying medicine when she joined Mother. She laughed: 'No, no,' she replied, 'Mother *made* me study medicine. You see, we used to go with Mother to get patients admitted to hospitals. They would not accept them. Even if we begged for clothes, bathed the poor, dressed them in nice clothes, hospitals were reluctant to take them. It was then that Mother said, "I want you to study medicine." I had been a good student in maths, but with all the disturbances in Calcutta I completed my matriculation in science. So I said to Mother that I'll do anything, but not medicine. Nor did I know much English. Mother got Michael Gomes to train me privately. She then sent me to Loreto House to study English. Every day she cajoled me by saying "try for one day more, one day more". Finally I was awarded my MBBS in the first division.'

We spoke about the early days. 'Did you beg for money?' I asked. 'It just came,' she replied. 'One day, I remember, we had no money, except for a little bit in a small box. It was a feast day and when Father Henry asked for a tiny contribution, Mother emptied the box. We had nothing left. You won't believe it but the very next morning when we went to mass to St Teresa's Church, a man gave Father Henry a hundred rupees for Mother Teresa.'

What was life in Creek Lane like, I inquired. Was there enough food to eat? Sister Gertrude went into peals of laughter at the very recollection. 'We never went hungry. Never. But the food we ate in the beginning, my God. Usually it was wheat germinated overnight in water. Father Henry had told Mother it was very healthy, but we could barely swallow it. That was for breakfast. For lunch we had boiled wheat with some salt. One day Charur Ma bought some cheap vegetables, which she boiled and boiled and all of us got sick. I only know that God had taken me by the hand, and I never thought of anything else.'

MOTHER TERESA SHEPHERDING HER COMPANIONS.

'I am an agnostic. I do not believe in God or any form of worship, but if there is a God I would say I found Mother Teresa's presence more divine than anything I had encountered before, because working for humanity is what to me is the basis of all religions and she is the one I know doing more than anyone else. I know lots of other people doing extremely good work, but I was very touched when, long after I had lost all contact with her after my cover story in Illustrated Weekly of India, of which I was editor, had appeared, she told a friend that one good thing that it had done was to dissipate the anti-missionary bias that pervaded Bengal. People no longer suspected that her only motive was to get converts to Christianity. She wrote me a letter ending with the sentence, "I am told that you don't believe in God but I send you God's blessings." I had this framed and it has a place of honour in my study in Kasauli.'

I asked him whether he believed she converted people to Catholicism. He replied without a moment's hesitation, 'I think it's a whole lot of hogwash. I was with her in the Home for the Dying in Kalighat. One person died in our presence. Everyone who stretched out his or her arm for help, she took it in her hands and the only words she used every time were Bhagwan Acchen, (there is God). She made them repeat it. I don't call that any kind of conversion; people died with God's names on their lips. I don't know when and how this canard of her converting people started. Even if we assume that she did convert, these are dying people. She was not adding to the number of Christians. As a matter of fact, I do happen to know that if people who died in the dying people's homes were Muslims they were buried; if they were Hindus they were cremated.'

KHUSHWANT SINGH

noted Indian writer and columnist, in conversation with Navin Chawla

MOTHER TERESA BEING GREETED IN TRADITIONAL MANNER DURING A VISIT TO THE NORTH-EAST OF INDIA.

GIRLS FROM ALL over the world apply to join the Missionaries of Charity. Many of them write simply that they want a life of poverty and sacrifice and desire to serve the poor. They come from many nationalities and from all levels of society. Some are very well educated and have completed their graduation or even post-graduation when they apply. The majority of the Sisters are Indian, causing Mother Teresa to say once, laughingly, that her Sisters were an Indian export item. No matter how difficult the work — and God knows it is difficult at the best of times — a smile is not far away from their faces. In their work, the only assistance is from volunteers; there is no porter or orderly to assist them, leading Mother Teresa to remark that in Calcutta they were known as the 'Coolie Sisters'.

NO MATTER HOW DIFFICULT THE WORK,

A SMILE IS NOT FAR AWAY FROM THEIR FACES.

The first recognition of her work, fourteen years after she began it, came from her adopted country. On 26 January 1962, in the customary list of honours announced on India's Republic Day, was the name of Mother Teresa, who had been nominated for the Padma Shri (the Order of the Lotus). This was the first time that a person not born an Indian was given this distinguished award. She was invited to go to New Delhi to receive it from the president. Her first impulse was reluctance, prompted by the conviction that she had done nothing to deserve it. It was the Archbishop of Calcutta who advised her to accept, as a recognition of the poor. In September that year she was ushered into the chandeliered Durbar Hall of the magnificent presidential palace, the Rashtrapati Bhavan. Earlier, eschewing the offer of a limousine to drive her from the convent, she drove past the resplendent president's bodyguard and cavalry in the ambulance-cum-general-purpose van of her Delhi mission.

Mrs Pandit, a former Indian high commissioner to London and sister of Prime Minister Nehru, was present that morning. She gave a vivid account of the ceremony. 'The sari-clad nun, a picture of humility, walked up to the dais. She took the award as if she was taking a sick child or a dying man in her arms. The hall went mad. There were tears in the eyes of the president. Later, when we were going home, I asked my brother, "Wasn't that a moving thing?" He said, "I don't know how you felt, but I had great difficulty in restraining my tears."'

Upon her return to Calcutta, Mother Teresa was to install the beribboned medal around the neck of a small statue of the Virgin, placed in a glass case at Nirmal Hriday in Kalighat. Not for a moment was she lulled into believing that it was she who was deserving. To this day, this first of innumerable honours adorns the statue of the one whom Mother Teresa believes is deserving of praise.

NAVIN CHAWLA
Mother Teresa, *Sinclair-Stevenson, London, 1992*

Receiving the Jawaharlal Nehru Award
for International Understanding from
Prime Minister Indira Gandhi.

'Why do we fear death?' I asked.

'There is no reason for that,' she replied. 'God has given us life and

when we die we go back to Him. We come from Him and return to Him.

The meaning of our lives is to do all we can for the glory of God and

the good of all people. Thousands have died with us, and I can only tell

you that none of them have been allowed to die alone and uncomforted.

Someone is with them, so that when they die, they die in peace.

MOTHER TERESA
in conversation with Navin Chawla, New Delhi, 25 March 1996

' We are called upon

not to be successful

but to be faithful. '

MOTHER TERESA

APPENDIX

As we have gathered here together to thank God for the Nobel Peace Prize, I think it will be beautiful that we pray the prayer of St Francis of Assisi, which always surprises me very much. We pray this prayer every day after Holy Communion, because it is very fitting for each one of us. And I always wonder that 400–500 years ago when St Francis of Assisi composed this prayer, they had the same difficulties that we have today, as we compose this prayer that fits very nicely for us also. I think some of you already have got it – so we will pray together.

Let us thank God for the opportunity that we all have together today, for this gift of peace that reminds us that we have been created to live that peace, and that Jesus became Man to bring that good news to the poor. He, being God, became Man in all things like us except in sin, and He proclaimed very clearly that He had come to give the good news.

The news was peace to all and good will and this is something that we all want – the peace of heart. And God loved the world so much that He gave His Son – it was a giving; it is as much as if to say it hurt God to give, because He loved the world so much that He gave His Son. He gave Him to the Virgin Mary, and what did she do with Him?

As soon as He came into her life, immediately she went in haste to give that good news, and as she came into the house of her cousin, the child – the unborn child – the child in the womb of Elizabeth, leapt with joy. He was, that little unborn child was, the first messenger of peace. He recognised the Prince of Peace, he recognised that Christ had come to bring the good news for you and for me. And as if that was not enough – it was not enough to become a man – He died on the cross to show that greater love, and He died for you and for me and for that leper and for that man dying of hunger and that naked person lying in the street not only of Calcutta, but of Africa, and New York, and London, and Oslo, and he insisted that we love one another as He loves each one of us. And we read that in the Gospel very clearly: 'Love as I have loved you; as I love you; as the Father has loved me, I love you.' And the harder the Father loved Him, He gave Him to us, and how much we love one another, we too must give to each other until it hurts.

It is not enough for us to say: 'I love God, but I do not love my neighbour.' St John says that you are a liar if you say you love God and you don't love your neighbour. How can you love God whom you do not see, if you do not love your neighbour whom you see, whom you touch, with whom you live? And so this is very important for us to realize: that love, to be true, has to hurt.

It hurt Jesus to love us. It hurt Him. And to make sure we remember His great love, He made Himself the bread of life to satisfy our hunger for His love – our hunger for God – because we have been created for that love. We have been created

in His image. We have been created to love and be loved, and He has become Man to make it possible for us to love as He loved us. He makes Himself the hungry one, the naked one, the homeless one, the sick one, the one in prison, the lonely one, the unwanted one, and He says: 'You did it to me.' He is hungry for our love, and this is the hunger of our poor people. This is the hunger that you and I must find. It may be in our own home.

I never forget an opportunity I had in visiting a home where they had all these old parents of sons and daughters, who had just put them in an institution and forgotten, maybe. And I went there, and I saw in that home they had everything – beautiful things – but everybody was looking toward the door. And I did not see a single one with a smile on their face. And I turned to the sister and I asked: How is that? How is it that these people who have everything here, why are they all looking toward the door? Why are they not smiling?

I am so used to seeing the smiles on our people, even the dying ones smile. And she said: 'This is nearly every day. They are expecting, they are hoping that a son or daughter will come to visit them. They are hurt because they are forgotten.' And see – this is where love comes. That poverty comes right there in our own home, even neglect to love. Maybe in our own family we have somebody who is feeling lonely, who is feeling sick, who is feeling worried, and these are difficult days for everybody. Are we there? Are we there to receive them? Is the mother there to receive the child?

I was surprised in the West to see so many young boys and girls given in to drugs. And I tried to find out why. Why is it like that? And the answer was: 'Because there is no one in the family to receive them.' Father and mother are so busy they have no time. Young parents are in some institution and the child goes back to the street and gets involved in something. We are talking of peace. These are things that break peace.

But I feel the greatest destroyer of peace today is abortion, because it is a direct war, a direct killing, a direct murder by the mother herself. And we read in the scripture, for God says very clearly: 'Even if a mother could forget her child, I will not forget you. I have curved you in the palm of my hand.' We are curved in the palm of his hand; so close to him, that unborn child has been curved in the hand of God. And that is what strikes me most, the beginning of that sentence, that even if a mother *could* forget – something impossible, but even if she could forget – I will not forget you.

And today the greatest means, the greatest destroyer of peace is abortion. And we who are standing here – our parents wanted us. We would not be here if our parents would do that to us.

Our children, we want them, we love them. But what of the other millions? Many people are very, very concerned with the children of India, with the children of

Africa where quite a number die, maybe of malnutrition, of hunger and so on, but millions are dying deliberately by the will of the mother. And this is what is the greatest destroyer of peace today. Because if a mother can kill her own child, what is left for me to kill you and you to kill me? There is nothing between.

And this I appeal in India, I appeal everywhere: 'Let us bring the child back'. And this year being the child's year, what have we done for the child? At the beginning of the year I told, I spoke everywhere, and I said: 'Let us ensure this year that we make every single child born, and unborn, wanted'. And today is the end of the year. Have we really made the children wanted?

I will tell you something terrifying. We are fighting abortion by adoption. We have saved thousands of lives. We have sent word to all the clinics, to the hospitals, police stations: 'Please don't destroy the child; we will take the child.' So every hour of the day and night there is always somebody – we have quite a number of unwedded mothers – tell them: 'Come, we will take care of you, we will take the child from you, and we will get a home for the child.' And we have a tremendous demand for families who have no children, that is the blessing of God for us. And also, we are doing another thing which is very beautiful. We are teaching our beggars, our leprosy patients, our slum dwellers, our people of the street, natural family planning.

And in Calcutta alone in six years – it is all in Calcutta – we have had 61,273 babies less from the families who would have had them because they practise this natural way of abstaining, of self-control, out of love for each other. We teach them the temperature method which is very beautiful, very simple. And our poor people understand. And you know what they have told me? 'Our family is healthy, our family is united, and we can have a baby whenever we want.' So clear – those people in the street, those beggars – and I think that if our people can do that, how much more you and all the others who know the ways and means can do without destroying the life that God has created in us.

The poor people are very great people. They can teach us so many beautiful things. The other day one of them came to thank us and said: 'You people who have evolved chastity, you are the best people to teach us family planning because it is nothing more than self-control out of love for each other.' And I think they said a beautiful sentence. And these are people who maybe have nothing to eat, maybe they have not a home where to live, but they are great people.

The poor are very wonderful people. One evening we went out and we picked up four people from the street. And one of them was in a most terrible condition. And I told the Sisters: 'You take care of the other three; I will take care of this one that looks worse.' So I did for her all that my love can do. I put her in bed, and there was such a beautiful smile on her face. She took hold of my hand, as she said one word only: 'Thank you' – and she died.

I could not help but examine my conscience before her. And I asked: 'What would I say if I was in her place?' And my answer was very simple. I would have tried to draw a little attention to myself. I would have said: 'I am hungry, I am dying, I am cold, I am in pain', or something. But she gave me much more – she gave me her grateful love, and she died with a smile on her face. Like the man who we picked up

from the drain, half eaten with worms, and we brought him to the home – 'I have lived like an animal in the street, but I am going to die like an angel, loved and cared for.' And it was so wonderful to see the greatness of that man who could speak like that, who could die like that without blaming anybody, without cursing anybody, without comparing anything. Like an angel – this is the greatness of our people.

And that is why we believe what Jesus has said: 'I was hungry, I was naked, I was homeless; I was unwanted, unloved, uncared for – and you did it to me.'

I believe that we are not really social workers. We may be doing social work in the eyes of the people. But we are really contemplatives in the heart of the world. For we are touching the body of Christ twenty-four hours. We have twenty-four hours in His presence, and so do you and I. You too must try to bring that presence of God into your family, for the family that prays together stays together. And I think that we in our family, we don't need bombs and guns to destroy or to bring peace – just get together, love one another, bring that peace, that joy, that strength of presence of each other into the home. And we will be able to overcome all the evil that is in the world. There is so much suffering, so much hatred, so much misery, and we with our prayer, with our sacrifice are beginning at home. Love begins at home, and it is not how much we do, but how much love we put in the action that we do. It is to God Almighty – how much we do does not matter, because He is infinite, but how much love we put in that action. How much we do to Him in the person that we are serving.

Some time ago in Calcutta we had great difficulty in getting sugar. And I don't know how the word got around to the children, and a little boy of four years old, a Hindu boy, went home and told his parents: 'I will not eat sugar for three days. I will give my sugar to Mother Teresa for her children.' After three days his father and mother brought him to our house. I had never met them before, and this little one could scarcely pronounce my name. But he knew exactly what he had come to do. He knew that he wanted to share his love.

And this is why I have received such a lot of love from all. From the time that I have come here I have simply been surrounded with love, and with real, real understanding love. It could feel as if everyone in India, everyone in Africa is somebody very special to you. And I felt quite at home, I was telling Sister today. I feel in the convent with the Sisters as if I am in Calcutta with my own Sisters. So completely at home here, right here.

And so here I am talking with you. I want you to find the poor here, right in your own home first. And begin love there. Be that good news to your own people. And find out about your next-door neighbours. Do you know who they are?

I had the most extraordinary experience with a Hindu family who had eight children. A gentleman came to our house and said: 'Mother Teresa, there is a family with eight children; they have not eaten for so long; do something.' So I took some rice and I went there immediately. And I saw the children – their eyes shining with hunger. I don't know if you have ever seen hunger. But I have seen it very often. And she took the rice, she divided the rice, and she went out. When she came back I asked her: 'Where did you go, what did you do?' and she gave me a very simple answer: 'They are hungry also.' What struck me most was that she knew – and who are they?

A Muslim family – and she knew. I didn't bring more rice that evening because I wanted them to enjoy the joy of sharing.

But there were those children, radiating joy, sharing the joy with their mother because she had the love to give. And you see this is where love begins – at home. And I want you – and I am very grateful for what I have received. It has been a tremendous experience and I go back to India – I will be back by next week, the 15th I hope, and I will be able to bring your love.

And I know well that you have not given from your abundance, but you have given until it has hurt you. Today the little children, they gave – I was so surprised – there is so much joy for the children that are hungry. That the children like themselves will need love and get so much from their parents.

So let us thank God that we have had this opportunity to come to know each other, and that this knowledge of each other has brought us very close. And we will be able to help the children of the whole world, because as you know our Sisters are all over the world. And with this prize that I have received as a prize of peace, I am going to try to make the home for many people that have no home. Because I believe that love begins at home, and if we can create a home for the poor, I think that more and more love will spread. And we will be able, through this understanding love, to bring peace, be the good news to the poor. The poor in our own family first, in our country and in the world.

To be able to do this, our Sisters, our lives have to be woven with prayer. They have to be woven with Christ to be able to understand, to be able to share. Today, there is so much suffering and I feel that the passion of Christ is being relived all over again. Are we there to share that passion, to share that suffering of people around the world, not only in the poor countries? But I found the poverty of the West so much more difficult to remove.

When I pick up a person from the street, hungry, I give him a plate of rice, a piece of bread. I have satisfied, I have removed that hunger. But a person that is shut out, that feels unwanted, unloved, terrified, the person that has been thrown out from society – that poverty is so hurtful and so much, and I find that very difficult. Our Sisters are working amongst that kind of people in the West.

So you must pray for us that we may be able to be that good news. We cannot do that without you. You have to do that here in your country. You must come to know the poor. Maybe our people here have material things, everything, but I think that if we all look into our own homes, how difficult we find it sometimes to smile at each other, and the smile is the beginning of love.

And so let us always meet each other with a smile, for the smile is the beginning of love, and once we begin to love each other, naturally we want to do something. So you pray for our Sisters and for me and for our Brothers, and for our co-workers that are around the world. Pray that we may remain faithful to the gift of God, to love Him and serve Him in the poor together with you. What we have done we would not have been able to do if you did not share with your prayers, with your gifts, this continual giving. But I don't want you to give me from your abundance. I want that you give me until it hurts.

The other day I received $15 from a man who has been on his back for twenty years and the only part that he can move is his right hand. And the only companion that he enjoys is smoking. And he said to me: 'I do not smoke for one week, and I send you this money.' It must have been a terrible sacrifice for him but see how beautiful, how he shared. And with that money I brought bread and I gave to those who are hungry, with a joy on both sides. He was giving and the poor were receiving.

This is something that you and I can do – it is a gift of God to us to be able to share our love with others. And let us be able to share our love with others. And let it be as it was for Jesus. Let us love one another as He loved us. Let us love Him with undivided love. And the joy of loving Him and each other – let us give, now that Christmas is coming so close.

Let us keep that joy of loving Jesus in our hearts, and share that joy with all that we come in touch with. That radiating joy is real, for we have no reason not to be happy because we have Christ with us. Christ in our hearts, Christ in the poor that we meet, Christ in the smile that we give and the smile that we receive. Let us make that one point – that no child will be unwanted, and also that we meet each other always with a smile, especially when it is difficult to smile.

I never forget some time ago about fourteen professors came from the United States from different universities. And they came to Calcutta to our house. Then we were talking about the fact that they had been to the Home for the Dying. (We have a home for the dying in Calcutta, where we have picked up more than 36,000 people only from the streets of Calcutta, and out of that big number more than 18,000 have died a beautiful death. They have just gone home to God.) And they came to our house and we talked of love, of compassion. And then one of them asked me: 'Say, Mother, please tell us something that we will remember.' And I said to them: 'Smile at each other, make time for each other in your family. Smile at each other.'

And then another one asked me: 'Are you married?' And I said: 'Yes, and I find it sometimes very difficult to smile at Jesus because He can be very demanding sometimes.' This is really something true. And there is where love comes – when it is demanding, and yet we can give it to Him with joy.

Just as I have said today, I have said that if I don't go to heaven for anything else I will be going to heaven for all the publicity because it has purified me and sacrificed me and made me really ready to go to heaven.

I think that this is something: that we must live life beautifully, we have Jesus with us and He loves us. If we could only remember that God loves us, and we have an opportunity to love others as He loves us, not in big things, but in small things with great love, then Norway becomes a nest of love. And how beautiful it will be that from here a centre for peace from war has been given. That from here the joy of life of the unborn child comes out. If you become a burning light of peace in the world, then really the Nobel Peace Prize is a gift of the Norwegian people. God bless you!

OSLO, NORWAY, 1979